A HARVEST
OF
MEMORIES

A HARVEST OF MEMORIES

- A Lifetime in Manx Farming

Harvey Briggs

The Manx Experience

Published by

The Manx Experience
45 Slieau Dhoo - Tromode Park - Douglas - Isle of Man - IM2 5LG

Copyright © Harvey Briggs and The Manx Experience 2002

ISBN No 1 873120 53 2

Inset picture on front cover:
John Costain from Foxdale, ploughing with his 1947 Ferguson TE20 tractor and International trailer plough of similar age.
John is the Manx champion ploughman with vintage equipment and among the best in Britain in this class.

Printed in the Isle of Man
by
Mannin Media Group Limited
Media House - Cronkbourne - Douglas - IM4 4SB

FOREWORD

by
The Honourable Noel Q. Cringle,
President of Tynwald

It is with the greatest of pleasure that I write this Foreword for Harvey's book. Over many years, Harvey's columns in the island's newspapers have served as wonderful links between town dweller and countryman.

His excellent narrative has brought alive to his readers what those involved in agriculture tend to accept as almost mundane. The natural world of animals, with their sometimes human-like behaviour, has been shared amongst us all via a lifetime's knowledge of pleasure and trauma. The vicissitudes of the never-ending struggle with our fickle climate have meant a sharing and empathy across the whole nation.

Today, our Island's agriculture not only faces a new century and millennium, but also a major shift from production-led support to acting in harmony with the environment. The timeliness of this book will show that whenever facing change, the indomitable spirit of a true countryman shines through.

I am pleased to be counted as a personal friend by Harvey and I know that any reader of this book will find it not only nostalgic but also very illuminating and educational. Chronicling as it does a lifetime from young farmer to farm labourer on a family farm to ultimately farming with Laura on their own account, this book is a masterpeice in tracing the major change our industry has witnessed in the second half of the last century.

In his own inimitable style, Harvey Briggs has provided for us an immense record that will be enjoyed either as a source of reference or for what it really is - a jolly good read!

Noel Q. Cringle

To my wife Laura,
whose support and
enthusiasm I have
relied upon for
over 50 years

INTRODUCTION

I was born in Ludlow, Shropshire, in 1920 and a year later went to live with older cousins in Burnley in Lancashire. My mother, who was unmarried when I was born, had trained in dairying and worked as a cheesemaker on a Cheshire farm.

I had been born during the euphoric rejoicing which marked the end of a long and horrific war. My father returned from it suffering from the effects of gas poisoning in the trenches, but I never knew him.

To have a child outside of marriage carried a terrific stigma in those days. Perhaps to escape the scorn of others, in 1922 Gladys Davies, as she then was, applied for and was appointed to a post with the newly-formed Isle of Man Dairies Ltd. in Spring Gardens, Douglas. As a result she became the first factory cheesemaker on the Island, and was the virtual founder of the Manx cheese industry. It is now carried on in the modern creamery at Cronkbourne, ironically enough built on the farm my mother lived on from 1923, and where I lived from 1926 until we both moved out in 1938.

In 1923 my mother married a Manx farmer, James McCubbin of Ballaslig, on the road from Douglas to Port Soderick. He was one of the farmers who brought milk to the Isle of Man Dairies by horse and trap. They took on the tenancy of the 80-acre Ballabeg Farm at Cronkbourne – today entirely built over.

In 1926 I came to live with them, and was immediately accepted by the people of the district. I walked to Braddan School with 30 children from Cronkbourne and the adjacent farms and cottages, where country life was still primitive and free from the distractions of television, radio and the motor car.

I loved the farm and thought of little else as a career, except for a brief diversion when I was 16. I acquired some religious fervour brought on by attending Braddan Church three times every Sunday and listening to the Reverend (later Canon) W.A. Rushworth, its vicar.

By that time I was one of those men and boys collecting pennies and halfpennies – even the occasional sixpence – from the many thousands of holidaymakers who thronged the open air services on a Sunday morning in summer.

'What are you going to do when you leave school?', a pious churchwarden asked me as we stood together one day, rattling our collection boxes at the gate at the bottom of Braddan Old Churchyard. 'I would like to go into the church', I replied with enthusiasm. 'What?', he retorted. 'You must be mad. We don't like bastards in the Church of England!'

It was the first intimation I had that I was illegitimate. Apparently the woman I called Auntie Gladys – later Gladys McCubbin – was my mother, and I had been born out of wedlock. None of my true friends, who must have known, had ever mentioned the fact.

The incident put me off organised religion for a long time although I have remained, I hope, a Christian all my life and cannot go to sleep without saying my prayers. I know that the God I pray to is more understanding and forgiving than some of His servants on earth.

On a happier and rather immodest note, let me state that I knew I was recognised as Manx when I was voted a life member of the Royal Manx Agricultural Society, the Manx National Farmers' Union, the Eastern Young Farmers' Club and the YFC Federation, and appointed Captain of the Parish of Onchan, the only non-Manx born Captain among the 17 at present. And I married a Manx girl, Laura Kermode, in 1951.

I think I will be staying.

I am indebted to Valerie Cottle for skilfully editing this book, to Hampton Creer for historical research, to Lionel Cowin and Jo Overty and other colleagues at Isle of Man Newspapers (in which some of the material originally appeared) for their encouragement, and to Mary Doyle and Rachel Turner for transcribing my copy.

Finally I must remember Gordon Kniveton, a life-long friend, who during his tenure of the publishing company, The Manx Experience, frequently asked me to write a book. I always pleaded that I was too busy with my farming and my journalism. It was just three days before his sudden and untimely death that I finally agreed to do so.

Fortunately for me, Colin and Gwynneth Brown, who had previously taken over the publishing company, shared his enthusiasm and, with their daughter Tracey, helped with the preparation of the book and looked after the overall publication.

Stephen Carter has kindly lent me photographs of the steam era from his private collection.

Finally, along with the publishers, I am indebted to Noel Cringle, President of Tynwald and a friend of many years standing for his kind Foreword to the book and for his suggestion for a title - which we all thought most appropriate!

Harvey Briggs

1
LEAVING THE GRIME BEHIND

Forests of tall chimneys belching black smoke, knockers-up with long poles tapping bedroom windows to disturb the dreams of the mill workers who, half an hour later, drummed on the cobbles with their iron-clad clogs on their way to a 6am start, were my earliest memories of life.

Although born in Ludlow, Shropshire, I lived with cousins in Burnley in Lancashire, one of the great cotton towns, until family circumstances brought me to the Isle of Man in 1926 to live with an uncle on a traditional Manx farm.

Up to then, after five years in Burnley, I thought the world was made of smoke. In an east wind dense clouds of it from industrial Lancashire drifted across the Irish Sea to blacken the fleeces of sheep in the Isle of Man, a fact I became aware of some years later.

On my journey to Douglas through Liverpool there was even more smoke, this time from the two funnels of the coal burning *SS Manxman* of the Steam Packet fleet.

It was still the age of horses and when we docked alongside the Victoria Pier my elder cousin, Hilda Briggs, hailed a landau pulled by one horse to take us to Ballabeg. The driver set off and on reaching the Quarterbridge headed south towards Spring Valley. He must have thought he had a wealthy fare who was willing to pay for the journey to Ballabeg in Arbory.

But Hilda, who had been to Ballabeg Farm, Cronkbourne, before, directed him to the correct destination and the horse trotted gently towards Braddan

Always the poser! With three friends the night before I left Burnley for the Isle of Man. The photograph was taken in an allotment opposite my home in Every Street. I'm the shy one on the right.

Bridge and up past the school. It was July 3rd, 1926, a lovely sunny day and we had moved out of the smoke.

I still remember the sweet smell of the hay as my uncle and his man built rucks (small round stacks) in the front field of Ballabeg Farm.

Although 'Balla' means farm or place, and 'beg' is Manx for small – so there is no need for the addition of 'farm' – we always used the word, otherwise our post went south to the village of the same name.

If I left behind the grime of a smoky cotton town, with it went the wonderful friendliness of the people. No one had much money except the powerful mill owners in their luxurious mansions hidden behind high brick walls with iron spikes on top to keep out intruders.

My cousins, Hilda and Edna, had been content with their wages as weavers. They could each operate six looms at a time, which gave them a couple of bob more than those with two or four looms. I often used the story that I had lived in every street in Burnley, a large town by any standard.

I could do so because Every Street was its name, a typical Coronation Street with people wandering in and out of each other's houses, helping when needed. The men drank in The Old House at Home, equivalent of the Rover's Return.

Life was very different in a district in the heart of the Manx countryside, even if it only took half an hour to walk into town. The same friendliness among neighbours ruled even if houses, except for those in Cronkbourne Village, were often isolated.

Young as I was, I knew on leaving Burnley that Britain was in the throes of the aftermath of the general strike, when the country came near to bloody revolution, as Russia had done a few years previously.

The miners continued to strike throughout Britain and even at the age of six I noticed the difference between capitalists and workers. For many years afterwards I regarded myself as a Socialist – until we bought our own farm in 1964 and I changed my colours!

There was a striking contrast between life at Coal Clough Council School in Burnley and Braddan School. In Burnley all the boys wore jerseys and all the girls pinafores, although there was no school uniform.

At Braddan boys and girls came to school in all sorts of clothes, most of them well-patched and often ill-fitting because they were handed down from older children in the family. To save on shoe leather in summer, some lads went barefoot.

I can never remember anyone being brought to Braddan School in a motor vehicle although sometimes on a wet morning drivers of bakers or milk vans would give us a lift, imploring us not to tell their bosses or they would be sacked.

Braddan School in the 1920s was away in the country with only one building nearby. Opposite was Tom Moore's Ballafletcher Farm, one of three of the same name adjacent to each other.

Mr. Moore had a small acreage on which he grew potatoes, vegetables and fruit for a retail round with a horse and float in Douglas. We watched him drive off before knocking on the farmhouse door to buy an apple. He charged us one penny each but his wife would let us have a rosy red for a half-penny.

Bill (Spud) Moore, a thorn in the flesh of politicians through his public speaking skills acquired at the Dilettanti Debating Society in Douglas, was his son and took over the business in later years using a motor van for deliveries.

John W. Gelling was the schoolmaster with two other teachers, Miss Moore and Miss Lace.

He instilled in me a love of all things Manx, perhaps easier to do with a 'comeover' than in a native born child who takes so much for granted.

Above all Braddan School taught us the three Rs – reading, writing and arithmetic – which would stand us in good stead all our lives. There was no electricity laid on and on a dark, winter's afternoon the children were sent home soon after 3pm to enable us to walk home in daylight, anything up to four miles. The

The author in his best suit and on his best behaviour.

hanging oil lamps in the school were never lit that I can remember.

I was a bit late starting to experience being given a day off school for Braddan Ploughing Match, one of the biggest events of the year, but Mr. Gelling let us out of school around 2pm in time to see some of the ploughing, followed by the horse parade at 3.15pm.

It was particularly exciting when the 1927 match was held at my home, Ballabeg Farm, in the field opposite Cronkbourne Village. It was all horses then because there were only about 10 tractors in the whole of the Isle of Man.

Now in my possession are the minute books of the defunct Braddan Ploughing Society. In them Mr. Gelling is commended for allowing the children to attend the match although the Education Authority had decreed that schools must no longer close for the local match. The last Braddan match was held at Ballamillaghyn at Mount Rule in 1934.

A highlight of those years was a journey on a bus outside Douglas, which had its own buses and cable cars for public transport.

Soon after the Manxland Company began running a service in June 1928, my aunt and I were in the town for the usual Saturday afternoon visit. We had walked into Douglas but returned home by bus which we boarded in Lord Street, where buses for the main towns and villages were lined up nose-to-tail.

We alighted at Braddan Bridge after a short but exciting journey of around two miles, and walked home to Cronkbourne. Until then we walked everywhere, apart from an occasional longer trip by pony and trap. There was no motor vehicle on the farm before 1939.

Braddan Bridge had another significance in that the accommodating Mr. Gelling allowed us out of school to see the TT races on the Monday and Wednesday each year. Only on Friday, senior race day, was the school closed.

We ran down to see our heroes ride by, each lad identifying himself with one of them. Speeds were so low that the flag marshal standing at the Jubilee Oak blew a whistle when a rider came around the Quarterbridge. This alerted a marshal standing opposite Braddan Church to stop the flow of people coming up the steps from the railway station and wanting to cross the road.

The races were the only occasion the trains stopped at Braddan Bridge, except for the open air church services held each Sunday morning in summer. Thousands flocked to Kirk Braddan by two or more special trains, charabancs, horse-drawn landaus and hackney vehicles. Even more walked, filling the road hedge to hedge, from the Quarterbridge or strolling through the Nunnery grounds. After the winters when we saw few strangers it was exciting to meet so many new people.

My school friend, Leslie Kissack, later to lose his life with the Manx Regiment in Crete in 1941, and I were camping as 14-year-olds in the garden of his mother's house, Ivy Dene, adjoining Braddan Church one Sunday night.

Around 2am we heard noises near the church.

Could it be ghosts stirring in the old churchyard? We were scared stiff and quickly left our tent and sought the safety of Leslie's house.

Next day we were interviewed by the police and were even more scared. A policeman cycled to our homes to talk to us separately about our recollections of the noises. It seems that burglars had broken into the church hall and made off with the takings from the collection plates amounting to many hundreds of pounds. After that, someone at the office of the Isle of Man Bank, in those days before night safes, was on hand to receive the money every Sunday afternoon.

Cronkbourne was a community in itself. It had a social life in the village centred around Clucas's Laundry, which was owned by Tossie Clucas, later an MHK for Middle, and his brother, Stephen.

They brought electricity and piped water to Cronkbourne, inspired Braddan Football Club and began a badminton club in the laundry.

The Christmas tree and concert in 'Little Braddan', a one time chapel of ease at the top of the front street, was one of the most eagerly anticipated events. There would be a present for every child in the district, including, in 1926, one for 'the little boy from Ballabeg Farm'. They did not know my name but were aware of a newcomer in their midst.

Some of that special Cronkbourne community of 70 or more years ago survive and still meet, sadly these days, most often at funerals.

2
SHEEP PAID THE RENT

'Going to work on a farm? Well, there are worse jobs, but you haven't been very fair keeping out another boy who could have made more of his time here', my form master said when he asked me what I was going to do now that I was leaving school.

It was July 1936, the last day of my five years at the Douglas High School at St. Ninian's. 'Nobby' Clarke was a good teacher, but he berated me in front of the form for having no greater ambition than to become a farmer.

There was no secondary education except for a favoured few. Most children left primary school at 14, but there was a chance for a few to go to the high schools for boys at St. Ninian's, girls at Park Road, both in Douglas, and for boys and girls at Ramsey Grammar School.

Would-be high school pupils sat a written 11-plus examination. Four of us from Braddan School took the exam one Saturday morning in May 1931. Two were awarded scholarships, and my result was just good enough to give me a place provided my family paid six guineas (£6.30 in today's money) per year.

My uncle, with whom I lived, agreed, but two years later money became so scarce on the farm that I was almost taken away from school, as could legally be done because I was now nearly 14. He always maintained that 1933 was the year Manx agriculture hit the depth of its eight years of deep recession.

On his mixed farm at Cronkbourne in Braddan his income came from milk sales to customers in the village and to the Isle of Man Dairies in Spring Gardens, Douglas, potatoes, vegetables, eggs, oats, hay, a few store cattle and prime lambs from a flock of 40 breeding ewes. The 50 or so lambs were sold during summer to a Douglas butcher supplying meat from his shop to housewives all year around, but with a doubling in the weekly demand during the tourist season.

The butcher was Fred Brew in Castle Street. Mr. Brew would come out to our farm on a summer's evening once the shop was shut to buy lambs.

He did not drive himself and his nephew Fred Teare, who later took over the shop and died in 1999, was at the wheel of the van. Fred and I would stand aside as Mr. Brew and Uncle Jim haggled over the price of each lamb, a protracted affair with many insults flying, until a couple of hours later they shook hands and parted the best of friends.

The lambs would be marked for collection in due course when they were taken to Mr. Brew's own slaughter house in Lake Road, Douglas, or to holding fields he rented at Spring Valley.

The money for the lambs was held by Fred Brew, and used to pay off a contra account run up by my aunt for meat for the house. Any surplus in my uncle's favour was kept to help pay the farm rent in November.

In the summer of 1933 Mr. Brew's visits to the farm became fewer. Soon word got around that the Island's

At the waterfall on the Tromode Road near Cronkbourne village with my best friend, Jack, and wearing my first pair of long trousers. No boy went into them intil he was fourteen.

butchers, working together, had found a cheap supply of prime lamb in Stanley Market in Liverpool and were not buying locally. Furthermore, the boarding houses and hotels only needed legs or shoulders of lamb and the Manx butchers could order just these from Liverpool instead of buying the whole lamb from farmers and being left with unsaleable meat from the poorer cuts.

Meanwhile Manx lambs were 'eating their heads off' consuming grass needed for other animals.

Hearing that sheep were a 'middlin' trade' in Ramsey Mart, four Braddan farmers decided to pool their mature lambs and take them to Ramsey Mart on August Bank Holiday Monday, when the Island had its peak of visitors needing to be fed.

It was a day of great excitement for me as with a couple of other teenage lads I drove 40 lambs along the roads to Union Mills railway station for loading into a stock wagon attached to the noon train from Douglas to Ramsey via St. John's.

It was a special treat during those school holidays because we were allowed to accompany the lambs to Ramsey and given 2/- each to buy a meat pie, bread and butter, a cup of tea and a fancy cake in Bruce's Cafe opposite the mart in Bowring Road.

The farmers who gave us the money might not have been so generous a couple of hours later. As we drove the lambs into the pens in the mart we met farmers coming out. 'There's no point in taking them in', they called to my uncle. 'The butchers are not buying and most have gone home'.

However, a few were still there, sitting on the forms within the auction ring kept specially for them. No farmer ever dared to intrude on this privilege.

The lambs ran into the ring, glad to be released from the confinement of the railway truck. Alfred Chrystal, father of later auctioneers Fred and Turner, scoured the ringside for bids. The few butchers remaining, sensing a bargain, shook their heads, indicating that unless Mr Chrystal dropped his asking price they were not interested. None of the farmers wanted them either; they were sellers not buyers.

'Sorry men, I can't help. You'll have to try another day', Mr Chrystal said.

We had time for our meal at Bruce's Cafe before loading the lambs on the train for home. Those lambs stayed on our farm until October when, in desperation, my uncle 'gave them away' as he said because he needed the money for the rent and what grass they had left for other sheep and for the horses and cattle.

Ballabeg Farm, adjoining Cronkbourne Village,

14

covered 80 acres of fertile soil all within a ring fence. Now it has grown a crop of buildings comprising two abattoirs, a creamery, a factory, a vehicle testing station and in its upper reaches, the new hospital, as well as the Millennium oakwood.

In the days before I left it in 1938, one of its assets was its proximity to a market for food in nearby Douglas. Transport was mainly by horse so outlying farms were at a disadvantage in making deliveries. This meant that our landlady, a Mrs. Graham living in Quarterbridge Road, could ask a rent of £3 per acre for a farm in Braddan compared with £2 in most other parts of the Island. But that extra £80 took some finding each year and we grew four acres of potatoes for sale to Bill Kelly, who had a 'spud round' in Douglas, for our own deliveries to boarding houses, and for customers calling at the farm.

The potatoes were mostly of the early varieties for sale in summer. Each morning in July and August a ridge or two would be 'graiped' out, that is dug with a fork. Mechanical diggers were not yet successful and besides, it was better for my uncle to pay a pittance for an extra man than to spend money on implements.

Three or four men or lads picked the potatoes off the ground, sorting them into three baskets for 'good', 'rubbish' and 'seed', the latter to be planted for next year's crop. By 11am, each morning except Sunday, a float – a light cart – pulled by a pony would be on the road with bags for Bill Kelly and two grocers we supplied, Robert H. Kinley at the foot of Bray Hill and Edwin Cowley & Sons on Prospect Terrace.

Another daily chore, summer and winter, was milking our 18 cows by hand. They were mostly red, roan or white shorthorns, which also bred the young cattle needed for beef. In a mixed farming system everything had to be saleable, especially when prices were low.

Another market was supplying loads of loose hay and oats to the stables of tradesmen still relying on horses. Once a month from October to March, we delivered a cart load of turnips to the soup kitchen which provided the needy of Douglas with at least one good meal a day. Hard as times were for farmers, my uncle donated the last load of winter, free of the charge he made for the rest of the turnips.

Farm work was still done by horses on most farms. It was to be 1943 before we bought our first tractor. We kept three heavy horses for field work and a pony for the road. They were members of the family comprising Tiny (the biggest at 17 hands) Blossom and Prince, all Clydesdale, and Tommy, the smallest, called a half-legged because he was light boned and had speed as well as strength.

In spring Tommy would sometimes be called upon to make a second pair for field work such as harrowing or rolling. When Tiny, noted for his pulling power, dropped dead in the harvest field it was a terrific blow both emotionally and financially. Farm horses were scarce and expensive and my uncle could have replaced a working man easier than a working horse.

Within a few days we were joined by Billy, much lighter in build than Tiny. A black gelding, Billy was temperamental and prone to jibbing on a bad morning. My uncle bought him from Clucas's Laundry on the understanding that if they needed him for short periods he would be available on loan.

Billy had begun his working life on the streets of Liverpool before being brought to the Island by a dealer who sold him to Tossie Clucas, then developing the laundry at Tromode, that part of the district over the River Glass and in Onchan parish.

Although Billy's work had been pulling a cart to collect and deliver laundry in Douglas, he soon adapted to farm work finding pulling a plough with chains as easy as between shafts, where the horse carries the weight of the cart on its back. Our work in the fields with horses was governed by the hours of daylight in mid-winter but by February 12th it was ordained that we keep on ploughing until 6pm.

When we complained that our hours were supposed to be 6am to 6pm and that when we stayed longer in the fields we still had half an hour or more at work feeding and grooming our horses before we finished, we were reminded that in the dark days before Christmas we were often back in the stables before 4pm, waiting for tea-time. Overtime was unknown on farms, of course.

From 1936, when I left school, three men ran Ballabeg Farm: my uncle Jim McCubbin and the horseman Albert Sayle, while I took over more or less from the casual help employed before then. Like most farm lads of the time I was clothed, fed, had a bed in the farmhouse, and was given half a crown pocket money on a Saturday night.

The regular farm workers fared little better, but had the security of work and a home when so many others were on the dole or in the government's winter work schemes. Tourism was expected to provide a living for them in summer.

Farm men were expendable but hiring at Hollantide (November 12th) for a full year was honoured on both sides. Nevertheless, the horses often had a better time than the men. On a wet and stormy day the boss would say that it was too rough to take the horses out of the comfort of the stable, but he would order the men to find a sheltered hedge to trim

Blossom, our last working Clydesdale horse, on right, with Laura's grey riding pony, Punch.

in order to earn their wages. The only wet weather gear we had were two thick corn sacks; one we draped over our shoulders, the other we secured around our waists with binder twine.

However hard we worked during the week we always made our way from Braddan to Douglas on a Saturday night, usually on foot. There we would stroll through Strand Street to meet friends before going to the second house of the pictures.

We had plenty of choice of cinemas in those days, with the Picture House and Strand in Strand Street, the Regal in Victoria Street and the Royalty in Walpole Avenue. In the summer we could go to the Crescent on the promenade.

People always said they could recognise the country lads by their ploughboard walk. We tended to take long, economical strides to cover rough ground more easily when we were following the horses. They had to plough three quarters of an acre of land in a day, plodding 12 miles in the process.

The farmers' wives and daughters were known by their hats, adorned with imitation fruit and flowers. Perhaps we were the last generation of countrified characters. Today, in dress, language and behaviour, everyone seems the same.

3

THE GENTLE GIANTS

In 1936, when I left school, motor cars and vans were still few and far between on farms; on our farm we depended on horse transport until 1939. And it was to be 1952, when the government began its rural electrification scheme, before most country districts had a supply of electricity.

Until then – or even later in more remote areas – oil lamps of various kinds and the almost indestructible hurricane lamp, which could be carried around the buildings by its handle, were the only means of illumination apart from candles, which were used mainly in bedrooms.

A step forward was the appearance of pressure lamps, usually made by a firm named Tilley, which gave a brighter light than a paraffin lamp. The new lamps had a mantle and needed pumping by hand several times during an evening, but they saved the daily trimming of lamp wicks. Without regular attention the wicks smoked, polluting the atmosphere and blackening the glass through which the dim light shone.

There was nothing more ghostly on a dark winter's night than the sight of a man in the distance carrying a hurricane lamp and casting intermittent light and shadows as he strode over a field. He might be on his way to attend to a lambing ewe or calving cow or simply making a visit to a neighbour.

Eleanor Hunstill, who kept the village shop in the back street of Cronkbourne Village, supplied 'hard' groceries, as they were called. In her garden she had installed a tank containing paraffin for lamps. She impressed upon people to come for their quart or so in daylight because measuring it in the dark with only the light of a candle could create a fire hazard. Nevertheless those who had neglected to fill their lamps before dark were never turned away.

Mrs. Hunstill provided a new service around 1932, a daily newspaper. It was available about an hour after the 10.30am Steam Packet sailing from Liverpool arrived in Douglas, almost without fail at 2.50pm.

A regular order for a national daily had to be placed. The papers were delivered by a lad with a carrier bicycle to Mrs. Hunstill by McFarlane's, who had a newsagents shop in Prospect Terrace, Douglas, about two miles away. My family took the *News Chronicle* and I became an avid reader of news of farming further afield written by its agricultural correspondent, L.F. Easterbrook. But no-one ever bought a Sunday newspaper, because reading one on the Sabbath was against the teaching of both church and chapel.

In 1934 we had our first wireless set on the farm. It was a GEC bought from Harold Colebourn, an enterprising young man who foresaw opportunities in commercial business. At that time he had a loft somewhere in Upper Douglas where he repaired sets. Always the entrepreneur, he advertised second-hand wirelesses at very low prices.

My uncle, aunt and I walked to his workshop one Friday evening, and like most of his prospective pur-

A turnout from Messrs Forrester of Ballashamrock. Port Soderick at a Braddan Ploughing Match circa 1922. In the background is the mental hospital.

chasers finished up buying a brand new GEC set. We could have had a more sophisticated Murphy, but they were dearer, and even Mr. Colebourn with his salesmanship could not convince my uncle that it was worth the extra.

Most wireless sets (the word radio was rarely used before World War Two) ran on wet batteries, except when an electricity supply was available. Listeners would walk miles once a week to some spot with electricity where the run-down battery could be exchanged for a charged one. Our nearest point was Clucas's Laundry, now with electricity, which offered free charging to everyone in the district.

Again, there was a man of entrepreneurial skill because a Mr. Randle began a weekly round with a motor van supplying charged wet batteries. He took out the old battery from the back of the set, and replaced it with a charged one. He could be depended upon to arrive at the same time every week and we were never without sound. The business he founded is still operating in Glen Falcon Road, Douglas.

The dependence on horses for field work and road haulage continued to 1939, when we bought a second-hand Morris Oxford motor car, and 1943, when we acquired our first tractor, a Fordson with steel wheels.

When I was still at the Douglas High School, in the mid-1930s, I used to gaze through the window and watch John Looney and his son Billy lead two pairs of horses up Bray Hill, to plough and cultivate the fields on Tromode Park which then extended to Parkfield Corner. All that land is now houses.

The Looneys were the horsemen for Louis Callow, who farmed at Port-e-Chee with its extensive meadow. I wished that I was with them because my heart was in farming, not in maths, algebra, chemistry, science or sport, although I did enjoy Latin with Harry Carr, French with Norman Crampton, English with Billy Buck and history with George Shaw.

Out in the country there were still 1,296 farmers who employed 2,000 full-time workers and 770 part-timers. Now there are fewer than 600 farmers on 766 holdings, only 201 regular workers and 112 casuals. At their peak, working horses totalled 5,000; they have since been replaced by 1,277 tractors at the last count.

These horses needed shoes if they were in work, and every parish had at least one smithy. There were three blacksmiths in Braddan in my youth. Ned Carrooin was at the Strang, John James Kayes at the Cooil, and Bill Radcliffe at Union Mills.

From Ballabeg Farm we sometimes used the services of William Corkill, somewhere off Lord Street, on occasions when the horse was in Douglas making deliveries, but Ned Carrooin was our regular blacksmith. Often a horse would be taken there after midday dinner for shoeing, and I would lead it home after my day at Braddan School. I felt proud to be in complete charge of a huge Clydesdale, and they were all gentle giants.

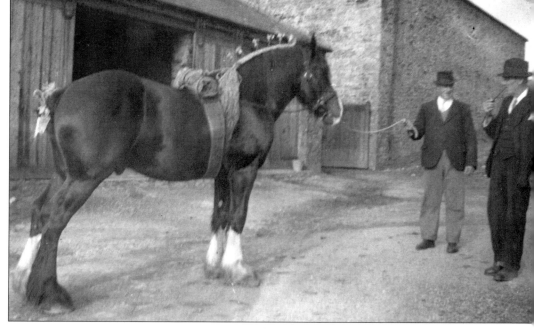

A Clydesdale stallion belonging to the Dalgliesh family of Ballawattleworth near Peel, prior to a season, from March to July, travelling the Island to mate with mares on farms.

Smithies needed to be within walking distance of farms. The blacksmiths – farriers nowadays – gave priority to shoeing horses. There were no telephones at either farm or smithy, and men with horses invariably turned up unannounced. When there were no horses to shoe, the smith was kept busy sharpening the points on harrow pegs, laying plough shares and coulters, hooping cart wheels or fixing farm implements. More than that, the blacksmith's shop with its fire and forge was the meeting place for the men of a district in the days when it was considered somewhat immoral even to enter a pub. In any case few men had any money to spend on drink.

One of the biggest advances of the 1930s was the introduction at an affordable price of the wellington boot. Before that, farmers and their men had worn hobnailed boots and leggings on the farm, with a pair of best boots and polished leggings for 'going out'.

Albert Sayle, the horseman at our farm, preferred puttees to leggings for work. They had been wartime issue to soldiers in 1914-1918, and consisted of a roll of canvas which was wrapped around the lower leg starting at the ankle and finishing below the knee where they were tucked in to keep tight.

None of these were waterproof, and a lot of time had to be spent cleaning off the mud they collected. 'Wellies' were marvellous. They kept feet and legs dry and could be swilled in a stream or under a tap. Their main disadvantage was that feet often sweated in them when men walked many miles a day after horses. So heavy leather boots were still needed for work in the fields. I kept a pair of wellies and a pair of hobnail boots in the stable and changed according to the work I had been allocated.

Nevertheless, wellington boots were a great advance on farms. Even women, usually picking their way through mud in skirts and shoes, turned to them for convenience. Women began to imitate men by wearing trousers, to the consternation of many men, although we had to admit that they were more practical.

Before long the Manx Women's Land Army would clothe members in riding breeches or overalls previ-

Robert C. Quayle, Ballacreggan, Port Soderick, with his prize-winning Clydesdale mare, Bess, at the Royal Manx Agricultural Show at Nunnery Park, Braddan in 1953.

ously worn only by men. Around the same mid-1930s, hand-held torches or bicycle lamps fitted with dry batteries provided convenient and instant light for walking or cycling in the dark.

In 1924, a commission chaired by Ramsey Johnson, later a deemster and the founder of the Manx National Farmers' Union in 1946, recommended that farm workers should finish work at 4pm on a Saturday rather than 6pm.

'We'll never get the field work done in time for spring sowing', complained Caesar Moore, a prominent farmer at Nunnery Howe, Braddan.

Nevertheless, the new hours were adopted and this enabled men to get to town a couple of hours earlier on a Saturday, to catch at least the second house at the pictures. They still had to work from 6am to 6pm five days a week, and every Sunday morning, with just every second Sunday afternoon 'off'.

Farmer and worker were still receiving scant reward for their labours, as the agricultural depression continued and foreign food supplied the Manx market.

'Farmers are squeezing the life blood out of their wives and children in their struggle to produce cheap food', declared Arthur Cottier, MHK for Ayre, in an impassioned appeal to Tynwald in 1934.

Tynwald listened, and even Gussie Craine, a Labour Party member representing a Douglas constituency, called for an end to the town versus country battle and appealed for support for the dying farming industry.

Tynwald passed its first Agricultural Marketing Act. This led to the setting up of a farmer-elected marketing society with satellite associations to deal with milk, fatstock and potatoes. The act also enabled the government to control the importation of basic foods such as meat, milk, eggs and potatoes when local supplies were sufficient. It proved a lifeline that saved a sinking industry.

4
NEW HOME, NEW JOB

'I've had a good offer from the government for your farm. I don't want to ask you to leave, but at least you have a few months to find another', was the unexpected bombshell which shattered the lives of our family at Ballabeg Farm in July 1938. The news came from Elizabeth Ellen Graham, our landlady, a lovable lady who always gave me half a crown whenever she met me. Needless to say I went out of my way to meet her.

Our 10-year lease on the farm still ran until Hollantide. The Isle of Man lagged behind the UK in adopting tenant security. The legal profession in Athol Street made sure of that; advocates lived on drawing up farm leases, and in the frequent litigation between landlord and tenant, 80% of Manx farmers were tenants, the remainder owner occupiers. Today the exact reverse is the case.

From the draconian lease my uncle signed on January 24th, 1925: 'The tenant shall cut off and leave upon the demised premises the tops and bottoms of all turnips grown thereon'.

A strict rotation of crops was imposed, with a seven-course system ordering a crop of oats in the first year, green crop in the second (when the land had to be properly cleaned, 20 cart-loads of farmyard manure and five hundredweight of bone manure applied to each acre), after which a corn crop was permitted in the third year, to be undersown with good English and Scotch rye grass and clover to make a pasture for a period of four years in grass. Throughout those seven years only one cut of hay (silage was virtually unknown in those days) was allowed.

The farm hedges, gates and ditches had to be maintained to the satisfaction of the owner. Any breach of the lease could result in an order to quit provided it was made before Tynwald Day (July 5th) with effect on November 12th.

Farmers observed that the men (there were no women advocates then) who drew up the leases had little experience of practical farming. For instance the insistence on leaving the leaves and roots of turnips in the fields was based on a misconception of the practice as a means of green manuring; in fact by the time the field was ploughed, up to five months later, all the residue had wilted and vanished. Nor did the inflexible rotation of crops allow enterprising farmers to try new methods.

Reluctantly, on advice from her lawyers, Mrs. Graham posted the notice which ordered my family's eviction from the farm no later than Hollantide Day. We began a hunt for a house and employment of some kind. When farmers have to leave their holding they lose their home and livelihood, and until 1969 there was no compensation for disturbance although it had been law in the UK for 40 years.

My uncle looked at the few farms available for renting but none suited, usually because of the high rent demanded.

Ballabeg farm house at Cronkbourne, where I lived from 1926 to 1938. It had been a mansion house for the Moore family of Cronkbourne and still had servants' quarters with a row of bells for summoning staff. Now, with the chimney stack removed, it is the only original building still standing on a once busy 80-acre farm, covered by two abattoirs, a creamery, numerous offices, the Government's vehicle testing station, the Millennium oak wood and its latest addition, the new headquarters building for the local publishing and printing operation, Mannin Media Group.

Buying a farm was out of the question, especially as the banks, the only dependable lenders of money, refused loans to a depressed agricultural industry.

We were being evicted – a strong word but truly applicable – because the Manx Government wanted the Ballabeg land to build a new hospital. Now, 63 years later, the hospital is under construction on the upper reaches of the farm. An apologist for today's civil servants says 'That is what is known as forward planning!'

In fairness to the government of the day, it was intended to use Ballabeg Farm as an extension of Ballamona Hospital Farm. Therapy for patients, mostly men but sometimes women too, included working in the fields, and the acquisition of Ballabeg would mean that it could be used in conjunction with another farm owned by the government, Ballafletcher, at the back of Braddan Cemetery.

As our leaving day loomed, my uncle arranged with auctioneer Jack Riley of Quine's Corner, Douglas, to sell all his live and deadstock – the name used for all the effects of a farmer apart from any land he may possess.

On Michaelmas Fair Day, the second Wednesday in October, we still had nowhere to live, nor any job in prospect. Unemployment was rife, and there were few prospects for a teenage lad like me. But just when we had given up hope of staying in farming and retaining the horses, cows, sheep and pigs we had built up since 1924, a farm became available for rent.

Ballakilmerton, as it was known until we changed it back to the original spelling of Ballakilmartin, was on offer following the appointment of its previous tenant, John Robert (Bobby) Gale, to be farm steward at the Board of Agriculture's Knockaloe Experimental Farm at Patrick. The rent for the 100-acre Ballakilmartin was £200, a reduction of £1 per acre on Ballabeg, which commanded more because it was nearer to the markets in Douglas in an age of slow horse transport. But there was an extra charge on our new farm, the tithe of £6 per annum – a lot of money then – collected 'to support the Crown and the clergy'. Tithe had once been applicable on every farm, but in most cases had been redeemed by a bulk payment. It remained unpopular with those farmers who had to pay it until it was finally abolished by Tynwald in 1946.

In 1938 we still didn't have a tractor, and all movement of implements from Braddan to Onchan was by horse. Only the corn binder, biggest of all our tackle, was moved by a neighbour with his tractor, a Fordson on rubber tyres.

Frank Clarke of Ballanard Farms had bought one of the first tractors in the district and offered to move the binder. He hitched to it at Ballabeg. 'I'll see you on my way back', he called to me as we prepared to move off together. I had a load of small equipment including a horse plough, a turnip cutter and a set of harrows, loaded onto a stiff cart with a Clydesdale gelding, Prince, in the shafts. I set off up Johnny Watterson's Lane, turned right at Willaston Corner, then left at Parkfield towards Onchan. When I reached the TT Grandstand I found Frank standing beside the tractor and binder. 'What's wrong?' I asked. 'The wheel bearings have overheated', he replied, and I saw smoke pouring from the wheel hubs, which had been made for slow-moving horses, not the faster tractor.

This incident, for me, marked a milestone on the change from horse to tractor power which was not achieved as smoothly as some may think. It took a lot of adjustment to adapt to mechanisation in agriculture.

Friday, November 18th 1938, was the main moving date. The 18 dairy cows would be milked by hand at Ballabeg in the early morning and at Ballakilmartin in late afternoon. Four teenage lads on bicycles, of which I was one, herded 40 cattle in all on the three-mile journey by road along the Ballanard Road to Parkfield Corner, then on through Douglas and Onchan to our new farm on the Whitebridge Hill.

But it was an easy trip. We encountered just half a dozen motor vehicles, all of which stopped in a long established custom when motorists met animals. Any houses with gardens protected them with fences or walls, and all had a gate. The lad in front made sure the gates were shut, two lads blocked the side roads, and I rode behind shouting orders like John Wayne on a cattle drive.

Livestock transport by motor lorry was still in its infancy in those days. Bob Teare at Sandygate,

A group proudly showing off a foal belonging to Douglas Corporation in its horse tram service. Identified are, on the left, Tom Joughin, blacksmith, and third from the left Stephen Strickett, one of the last men to work exclusively with horses.

Andreas, had bought the first specialist wagon in 1931, and he was followed as a livestock haulier by George Wade in Ballaugh and Fred Leece in Douglas.

Fred Leece was engaged to move one lame cow, a red Shorthorn named Winnie, and eight calves too young to walk the distance. Otherwise his Bedford lorry could carry only seven adult cattle, and moving the whole herd would have needed several journeys. It was easier – and cheaper – on foot.

On our way from Braddan to Onchan we passed 10 farms, each supporting a farmer and his family and two or three workers. Today all 10 have been submerged in houses to make the biggest conurbation in the Isle of Man.

5

ATTRACTING THE CROWDS

Farm auction sales until about 25 years ago ran to a dozen or more held over three weeks before and after Hollantide; they were often described as the farmers' wakes or holidays. November 12th marked the end of the farming year in terms of field work, with most crops gathered.

There was a welcome lull until it was time to begin preparations for another season of crops. Reasons for selling off might include a farmer carrying on no longer because he could not make a living, he might have come to the end of his lease and failed to renew it with the landlord, or he could be in the happy position of going into well-earned retirement.

Two days before we moved into Ballakilmartin, the former tenant, Bobby Gale, held a sale attended by an immense crowd of buyers and sightseers. I am indebted to Frances Corkill of Onchan for providing a complete sale list which Mr. Gale gave to her late husband, Bert Corkill, his nephew and from the family which founded Corkill's Garage.

The sale, on November 16th 1938, was conducted by Jack Riley, whose son, Raymond, continued the auctioneering side of Riley's of Quine's Corner, Douglas, now specialising in horticultural supplies under a fourth generation, Martin Riley. The auction realised a total of £1,418 from which had to be deducted (in pre-decimal currency) £23.13s. auctioneers' commission, £5.12s.6d for press advertising, £6.5s. for 2,000 buns for lunch, £1.10s. for two men to tend the boiler and make the tea and 7/6d for the hire of mugs. All implements were for horse draught.

An early Austin tractor on steel wheels was sold privately before the sale. It had been used for pulling the corn binder at Ballakilmartin, replacing the horses. The Austin must have been among the first to reach the Isle of Man; even by then the company had ceased making tractors to concentrate on motor cars. I understood at the time that it went to Mr. Gale's brother-in-law at Church Farm, Malew, but the family has no recollection of it.

Top price of the sale was £40.15s. for a brown Clydesdale mare sold to F. Kinrade. Seven horses in all included a meg foal reared on the bottle after its mother died. It was bought by Matt Clague and remained a family pet and working horse at Ballig Farm, just a couple of fields away from its place of birth. The only animal marked 'unsold' in the list was a colt foal, perhaps a sign that farmers were beginning to look to tractors instead of horses for field work.

Bobby Gale was a noted breeder of Dairy Shorthorn cattle and Suffolk sheep, winning many prizes at the two Manx summer shows. So the 25 milking cows met a steady trade, with John Fargher, Eyreton Farm, Crosby, paying £32.10s. for a newly-calved cow. An in-calf heifer was knocked down at £33 to Pete Kelly, Shenvalla, Patrick.

Another, described as a Christmas heifer, obviously being fattened for that market in November, was bought by Leslie Cowley, farmer and butcher at Baldromma Beg, Lonan, for £28.

Leading the pedigree Suffolk sheep was a pen of shearling ewes destined at a bid of £14.12s.6d for three to go to Knockaloe, Mr. Gale's new home, when George Howie bought them for the Board of Agriculture. The ram realised £5.7s.6d to Mr. Gale's neighbour and rival Suffolk breeder, George Piercy, of Bibaloe Moar.

In 1938 most fertilisers were sown on the land by a man dipping into a 'brat' (a sack hung around his neck) and broadcasting them as he walked across the field. But one UK farm, Bamfords of Uttoxeter, made a drill which dis-

Andrew Kennaugh in the handles of the plough from Ballatrollagh, Arbory and Johnny Russell of Douglas and Corlett Sons and Cowley Ltd., with a turnout they have made ready for the ploughing match season in the late 1940s.

tributed the fertiliser evenly from a box-like contraption on two wheels drawn by one horse in shafts. One of these made the top price among implements at £19.10s when it was bought by T. H. (Tossie) Cowin of Douglas fashion house fame who also farmed at Conrhenny on the Onchan/Lonan border.

A hay pole sold for £3.2s.6d. to Stanley Corlett of Glenville Farm, Onchan. It had been used until then on two farms, Ballakilmartin and Baldromma Moar, Lonan, under joint ownership between the Gale and Cottier families.

Stiff carts auctioned at £10 and £7.10s, a disc type corn drill at £9, a corn binder at £9, a horse rake and a reaper both at £6. Horse harness, soon to rot in many stables when the tractor age took over, was still in demand in 1938; sets of trap harness fetched £3 and

£2.17s.6d, and a cart saddle for heavy horses £2.10s. Of course the prices bore little relation to today's values and reflect the farming recession of the time. A year later war brought food shortages and an even greater scarcity of farm equipment, both of which led to higher prices.

That part of Braddan adjacent to Douglas was already becoming urbanised when I left it in 1938, but I did not expect to see the 80-acre Ballabeg Farm at Cronkbourne Village become the site for two abattoirs, a creamery, an engineering works, a vehicle testing centre, the Millennium oakwood, numerous offices and now, in its upper reaches, a new hospital, in my lifetime.

Onchan parish, to which I moved, was still in the heart of the countryside in those days, with 42 full-time farmers, a fact I can confirm from the number of notices I sent out when I became secretary of the parish branch of the Manx National Farmers' Union. Today perhaps 15 make a living from farming, wholly or in part.

Ballakilmerton, as it was once spelt, appears in the earliest manorial roll in 1511 and was then occupied by Fynloe McKerron, an ancestor of the Christian family who continued as owners under various forms of land tenure until they sold it in 1942. The oldest stone buildings were erected in the 1700s and a newer range from 1830 – a date carved with pride by some craftsman in a beam on the cowshed loft. The back road, described in documents in the Manx Museum as 'the great paved way', was a public highway until it was replaced by the White Bridge Hill, constructed around 1840.

We young people on the closely clustered farms of Onchan and its neighbouring parish of Lonan lived in harmony with the land. We expected little in the way of luxuries and were happy in a community which supplied all our needs. Although most of us were glad to see the end of plodding after horses and toiling in all the dust, grime and noise of threshing by steam engine, both brought many hours of pleasure in the right proportion.

Leading a pair of horses to the field on a lovely spring morning, hearing the lark singing as it spiralled skywards, and being startled by the raucous call of the corn crake against a background chorus of other birds made farming the best job in the world. The rest of the day would be spent in the close company of a pair of uncomplaining horses. Life still continued at their speed.

Mill days brought the company we lacked in our everyday lives, although to many of us working on our own was one of the attractions of farming. At intervals of three weeks spread throughout winter we would visit each other's farms to make up a threshing crew after the mill and baler pulled by a lumbering steam engine arrived in the haggard (stack yard), its driver and feeder (mate) legends in their own lifetime.

A mill day was a hard one for all the 15 or so men who gathered, but it was a social occasion too. Only the women who had to feed the hungry workers dreaded mill days.

It was a busy week when there were two 'socials' we could enjoy in the evenings. For us in Onchan and Lonan they would be at Baldrine, Abbeylands or Laxey. Occasionally a social evening would be held in Onchan but some of its newer residents were inclined to frown on 'govags' from the country and we never felt really welcome.

We walked or cycled everywhere during the week, but on Saturday nights we really lived it up by travelling to Douglas by bus. The fare from anywhere on the road to the Half Way House (now the Liverpool Arms) was 5d. single, 9d. return. The country lads and lasses still strolled through Strand Street to meet and

Tractors began to replace horses on farms during the war years and here is Laura driving one of the first to come to Ballaugh in 1942 - a Fordson - note the steel wheels.

Left: Lunch, as we called morning and afternoon breaks for tea and jam 'pieces' in the fields, was a happy occasion. This scene is from the harvest field at Ballamona Moar, Ballaugh in 1942 when my wife, Laura (then Kermode), was serving in the wartime Manx Women's Land Army. Left to right: horseman Louie Corkill, his wife Ena, Laura, Valerie Kneen (now Kissack and living in Australia) and the farmer and Valerie's father, Edward C. Kneen. Standing is Edward Kneen, senior, retired but helping out.

exchange the skeet, but times were changing; we lads found that if we wanted to impress girls we needed a few social graces, and the ability to dance was one of them. Dancing was actually cheaper at a time when we had to watch the pennies; if you took a girl to the pictures you were expected to pay for her, but you could always meet her 'inside' at the Palais de Danse in Strand Street where she would have gone with her girl friends.

But first of all we had to learn ballroom dancing in our local district, because travelling to Douglas for classes was not an option after a day on the farm, where we were lucky to finish by 6pm. Dancing was banned in Methodist halls; it was considered immoral to hold a girl in your arms during a waltz or quick-step, although you could play 'Kiss-in-the-Ring', to the tune of 'Silly Old Man', or 'Spin the Plate' where you could claim kisses to your heart's content. This led to much passionate embracing, the nearest a lad ever got to a girl in those days.

Once, in the Laxey Glen Methodist schoolroom, some of us began innocently doing the Palais Glide where a row of boys and girls drape arms over shoulders and perform a few repetitive steps in time to music from a piano. We were stopped by a chapel steward, and told to leave and not return until we had learned how to behave ourselves.

But there were no restrictions in church halls and we put on our best suits and shoes (these just taking over from boots for evening wear) to trip the light fantastic in Laxey and Onchan. The Calderbank twins, Beryl and Dilys, who are still around the village, performed miracles with lads more accustomed to a ploughman's gait.

The Palais became our Mecca, but there was a wider choice in summer, with dancing in the Villa Marina, Palace and Derby Castle ballrooms. When the last bus from Douglas stopped at Begoade Road (marked now rather mistakenly as the Road of the Priest's Farm) no fewer than 18 young people, mostly lads but with two or three lasses, would pour off it on their way home. All were from surrounding farms where they earned a living. Now the bus has no need to stop; the few young people left on those farms have their own cars and most of the people in the houses use the country as a dormitory, work outside of farming, and show scant interest in the life of the community.

In the 1930s Manx farming was still being run in a feudal fashion with the traditions of a trinity of three – landlord, tenant farmer and worker. Even those regarded as owner-occupiers often paid mortgages equal to a rent, but at least they had a sense of freedom outside the harsh leases tenants had to honour. 'It's worth a lot to be your own boss', was a saying of the day.

But few in Manx agriculture really were. The landowner imposed his will on the tenant, the tenant on his workers – who had no one below them except the animals they tended. But they rarely took their frustrations out on them. The bond between a man and his horses, his cows, his sheep and his pigs often kept him tied to the one farm for years, even a lifetime.

Rarely in this trinity did anyone rise to a higher level but many dropped down, such as the farmer who could not make enough to pay the rent and his workers or support his family. The only skill he knew was farming, and he would usually have to take a job as a farm worker, taking instead of giving orders.

Land tenure was based on that introduced by the Stanleys, Earls of Derby, when they owned the Isle of Man. It centred around the soil being properly culti- vated to ensure enough food even in bad years for farming. The Hollantide deadline, November 12th, was set for the start and finish of the farming year. Farms changed hands and farm workers changed farms on that day. Some security for the tenant farmer lay in the lease system, but not enough to prevent him having to leave the farm at the end of a lease, often a short-term affair. A new Agricultural Holdings Act of Tynwald in 1969 was to change that.

The worker had a job for a year at least, including a tied cottage for a married man or a home in the farm house if he was single. These arrangements were binding on both sides and were fine if everyone got on well, but there could be heartbreaks too.

Problems came for workers when they grew old and were not easily employable. They could be out on the street with no home and the only prospect the old age pension of 10/- a week when they reached 65. A sad inci- dent which sticks in my memory was meeting an old farm worker on the White Bridge Hill on Hollantide Night in 1948. He was carrying his few possessions wrapped in brown paper tied with binder twine: his hob-nailed work- ing boots, a couple of shirts, a change of underclothes, two pairs of stockings, a cut-throat razor and little else. He was dressed in his going-out clothes, clean but shabby.

'What's wrong?' I enquired. 'Oh, I didn't get fixed up at the fair and I've nowhere to sleep tonight. Do you think your boss would let me sleep in the loft?' he replied, near to tears.

I assured him he would and he stayed on the farm for a couple of months, sleeping in the hay and keep- ing warm in the heat generated by 18 cows in the cow- shed below the loft. He received his food in the house in return for helping on the farm, but my uncle was fully staffed and could not afford to pay him.

The Hollantide hiring fair was held on the morning of November 12th in the yard of the Adelphi Hotel at the top of Nelson Street in Douglas, whence it had moved from a field at the Quarter Bridge around 1920. Not 'kept on' by his former employer, the old man expected to be hired at the fair, but age was against him. As spring approached he eventually found a live- in job with a farmer in Santon.

A Douglas lad I knew who thought he would like to work on a farm when he left school, went along to the Hollantide Fair and was hired to a farmer at St. John's. A couple of years later I met him driving a bread cart in Douglas.

'Didn't you like farming?' I asked. 'Oh yes, I loved it,' he told me, 'but I couldn't stand herring for break- fast, dinner and tea. I stuck the year though, and only went home to my parents in Douglas three times in all'.

If a worker found a good farm with plenty on the table and an understanding boss he stayed there for years, becoming like a member of the family. Others were not so lucky, and moved annually after honour- ing the custom of 'taking the shilling' which bound a man to a farm for 12 months.

Those of us working on the land in 1938 might have thought life would never change, but soon we were to live through the greatest-ever upheaval in Manx farming, an industry which has outlived smug- gling, mining, fishing and tourism in its most thriving form. Doubtless it will still be here after the last finan- cial consultant has flown out of Ronaldsway . . .

6

BETTER OFF THAN HEROES

'Colonel Bogey' rang out over the Manx countryside in the summer of 1939. It came from the brass bands of the Territorial Army in camp at Bibaloe Moar, across the road from Ballakilmartin. The colourful presence of over 1,000 men in uniform brightened our lives, not least the invariable camp followers, both holidaymakers and local girls who used our fields and adjoining glens in which to await and entertain their soldier boyfriends.

It was in the canteen of the camp that I tasted my first glass of beer. Still in my teens and from a home where the only alcohol was port wine at Christmas, I was taken to the camp by our cowman Billy Kelly, a single man in his 40s, no big drinker himself but not averse to a couple of pints on occasions. As we came out of the canteen we met some friends of the Methodist persuasion who had signed the pledge never to touch strong drink. They promised not to split this time, but if ever it happened again . . . This added to the excitement of the occasion and I began to feel like a man of the world.

Billy – stone deaf as the result of coming off his bicycle on Summer Hill when he was a boy – and I had jumped over the hedge from our Big Garey where we were stooking corn on a hot summer's afternoon. Our excuse was that we had suddenly become very thirsty, but it must have been premeditated because Billy had money with him. Normally we never carried money in our working clothes except when we went with a horse and cart to Douglas to deliver produce or pick something up and the boss gave us a shilling, to be returned if not needed. The 'bob', a pen knife and a piece of string, were always carried by horsemen on missions off the farm.

A day or two later, on that memorable Sunday, September 3rd 1939, Britain and Germany were at war. Soon the Hallamshire Regiment from Sheffield marched off to a real war after all their peacetime exercises.

Our farm was one of the few with electricity at that time. It had been installed by Bobby Gale with the help of a friend, Herbert Corlett of Ballabeg Farm in Lonan. They used equipment from the old prisoner-of-war camp at Knockaloe to generate electricity to light the farmhouse, the stable and the cowshed, but there were no power points; an oil engine drove a dynamo which fed the current into a bank of wet storage batteries.

People came to see a farm lit by electricity, and we discarded some of our paraffin lamps in the dwelling house and the hurricane lamps for the buildings. But it was premature. Before long the light would wane of a winter's evening, and no amount of re-charging the batteries improved the supply. They had come to the end of their useful life and we decided that there were more important necessities in wartime than lighting equipment for a remote farm. So in 1942, after four years of new-found luxury, we returned to oil lamps and candles. It was to be another 10 years before the mains supply reached us.

The 346-acre Knockaloe Farm, south of Peel, had been a town for 30,000 aliens and their guards until 1919. It was bought by the Manx Government in 1923 'in order to further education in agriculture and to establish an experimental farm'. In 1928 the government appointed its first agricultural organiser, George Howie, and he was to live at Knockaloe and direct its operation. There had always been farmers who were progressive and used the best technical advice, but this was the first active encouragement provided by the government.

Feeding of livestock, for instance, was the subject of the board's first advisory leaflet published in 1932. It told how to balance the traditional feeding of turnips, hay, straw and grass with better use of oats, the main cereal grown on Manx farms. Balanced rations would produce more milk and meat, it advised. There were new techniques to help grow better crops, and Knockaloe became the breeding ground for pedigree cattle, sheep and pigs.

George Howie was not just the board's only advisory officer; he was secretary, too, of the Agricultural Marketing Society from its formation under an act of Tynwald in 1934. In 1935 he was joined by Douglas Kerruish as the first Manx Government veterinary officer responsible for animal health. By then Wilfred Halsall had succeeded Alfred Tyson as secretary of the Board of Agriculture, and these three civil servants helped to develop a pattern of farming at a time when the industry was undergoing exciting changes. Among the politicians Richard Cain was a leader in farming improvement.

I learned to drive in 1939 when my uncle bought a

George Howie, M.B.E., the Manx Government's first agricultural organiser, appointed in 1928, made a huge contribution to the development of the industry. He served until shortly before his death in 1963.

10-year-old Morris Oxford car, our first motor vehicle. We took out the front passenger and rear seats to make room for a load of six milk kegs or five bags of potatoes. Alf Cain, a friend in the motor trade in Douglas, taught me to drive over a few Sunday afternoons. When I was considered fit to go out on my own, he signed a form confirming my competence and I was issued with a licence by the Highway Board. To this day I have never taken a driving test. In 1940 the government introduced compulsory tests before anyone could obtain a driving licence.

We rarely used the car for pleasure, nor was I allowed it for anything unconnected with the farm's business. We used it to deliver milk to the Isle of Man Dairies roundsmen who stabled their horses in a building at the foot of School Road in Onchan, but the luxury of delivering milk by motor ended when, with wartime petrol rationing, we ran short of coupons and had to revert to a pony and float.

The coming of war led to the setting up of war agricultural committees in each of the 17 parishes. Around a dozen leading farmers in a parish, together with a secretary drawn from the only two Young Farmers' Clubs, Northern and Central, would be charged with overseeing food production.

The Isle of Man's dependence on imported food created a critical situation when the war at sea prevented supplies reaching the heavily bombed docks. A campaign with the slogans 'Plough for Victory' and 'Dig for Victory' encouraged farmers and gardeners to grow all the food their patch of land could produce.

'The War Ags' as the parish committees were called, obliged every farmer to plough up 30% of his land for cereals, including a proportion in wheat to replace the Canadian grain used for flour and bread making.

Although bread was never rationed in the Isle of Man it was often scarce, and long queues would form outside bakers' shops. Each sack of wheat had to be weighed as it came off the travelling threshing mill. The engine driver was required by law to count the sacks and make a weekly return to Government Office.

In another war, against rats (we called them nothing else in the countryside) which lived in the corn stacks and consumed a lot of much needed grain, it was decreed by law that a three-foot-high close mesh fence must be erected around the area containing the corn stacks and the threshing outfit on 'mill days'. The mill men carried the wire and stakes from farm to farm on the threshing mill or baler.

This suited the lads, who with pitchforks and sticks made sure no rat escaped. After all, we were paid 2d. per tail for each male rat or 6d. for every female when we delivered them to the government agent in our parish. Kills of up to 150 rats in a day were not unusual.

Food rationing began with sugar in January 1940, only three months after the outbreak of war. Twelve ounces a week per person did not go far. My aunt gave each of us living in the house a jam jar with our own weekly ration after she had taken out enough to pool for the milk puddings she served almost daily at midday dinner.

My jam jar was replenished each Friday when the groceries were delivered, but by Monday it would be empty again. With difficulty I stopped spooning sugar into my tea, little realising that sugar rationing would continue for 14 years. On the day it ended in 1954 I found I could no longer bear the taste of tea with sugar in it.

Sugar rationing was followed by tea, butter, cheese, sweets and chocolates, while luxuries like ice cream were prohibited completely. Butcher's shops were ordered to close for two days each week, but this failed to halt the consumption of meat; eventually customers were rationed to 1s.3d. worth of beef, lamb or pork for each member of a household. But poultry could still be obtained if you knew a friendly farmer.

To control the supply of meat animals, auctioneering of fatstock was stopped. To this day it has never been resumed and under the Manx Government's fatstock scheme all finished stock goes directly to the one market, the meat plant at Cronkbourne.

In 1940 fat animals still went to the three marts, Ramsey on Monday, Ballasalla on a Tuesday, or St. John's on a Wednesday. Instead of being auctioned as previously they were allocated from a farmer to a butcher. Two men, one representing farmers, the other the butchers, graded the stock according to quality. Private deals between farmer and butcher were forbidden, and all slaughtering was confined to two abattoirs, at Ramsey and Douglas. We never went short of food on farms because we had first call on milk, eggs, poultry, potatoes and vegetables, none of which were rationed by government.

Clothes rationing called for anyone buying new garments to surrender some of the coupons they had been issued. We all became shabby, and finding enough coupons for working clobber was a real problem. The blackout of all lights after dark added to our wartime work. Car lights and bicycle lamps had to be fitted with hoods to direct the beam towards the ground. Even the dim glow of a paraffin hurricane lamp was a risk, so we covered the lamp with a sack. Inevitably this could lead to a fire unless the user was vigilant. All buildings on the farm used after dark were fitted with blackout material on windows and, if necessary, in doorways.

Still, we were better off than the men and women who left the Island to fight, some never to return. We saw no heroics, no danger, no separation from loved ones, but on the other hand I have never worked harder, before or since. Farm staffs were depleted, casual workers almost unobtainable, and we were still farming with horses. Two men did the work of three and it was not until we bought our first tractor in 1943 that the pressure eased a little.

Those of us of military age had to register, but once it became apparent that we were regular farm workers, not just men taking up farming to escape the call up, we were told that we were in a reserved occupation and must stay where we were unless we heard differently.

Nevertheless we could not help feeling guilty as we watched our pals take the brunt of the war. We all lost friends; in my case Leslie Kissack from Braddan Bridge, who was killed manning a machine gun with the Manx Regiment in Crete, and Reggie Caley, who lost his life in an aircraft crash while serving with the RAF in India.

Apart from growing food, one way we could contribute to the war effort, was to raise money for charities. The young men and women of our district decided to put on a concert in Baldrine Methodist Hall in April 1942 in aid of the Red Cross, which was sending food parcels to prisoners of war in Germany and Italy. There were several topical sketches and a lot of singing, perhaps with more patriotic fervour than harmony, when we belted out 'There'll Always Be An England' and 'The White Cliffs Of Dover'. It was a great success at a time when there was little other entertainment, and was repeated a week later for those who had failed to gain admission to our 'premiere'.

We were delighted but a little deflated on this second night when the worthy chairman from Douglas looked around at the cast of 30 farm lads and declared: 'As I look at so many men of military age I am reminded of the army recruiting officer in the First World War who called at a farm in Lonan and saw a young man milking a cow. "Why are you not at the front?" he roared. The lad pondered for a moment before replying: "Because I find the milk is at the back, sir"'.

I suppose someone from Douglas, which was denuded of young men, would be surprised that there were so many still in the countryside, but of course we had a genuine reason, backed by the government, for being there. After all, had not the British Minister of Agriculture R. S. Hudson said in 1940: 'We are fighting for our lives. Every single farm must produce the maximum of which each field is capable. This war may be won by the nation which has the last week's supply of food'.

7
MY GAWD, YESSIR!

I was following a pair of horses pulling a plough, plodding along in the furrow, balancing the plough when it hit obstructions such as large stones and focusing on a job which needed all my concentration, when I became aware of a figure standing on the headland at the end of the furrow. It was a lad from the next farm. 'Hello', he called, 'have you seen anything of our sheep?'

'No, when did you miss them?' I enquired.

He scratched his head before telling me: 'We didn't miss them until they were gone, boy'.

Arty was one of the men who made the countryside so rich and diverse in character in those days, compared with today when after watching the same television, listening to the same radio and reading the same daily newspapers, we are all much of a muchness.

Another farm man shook his head and declared on a cold, wet morning when I was feeling particularly miserable and bad tempered: 'My gawd, yessir, you're looking mighty *treih*. You know, unless you die laughing you'll be an ugly corpse'.

Farm hands were reckoned to be the lowest-paid workers in the Island. Billy Kelly, our cowman, was hired for a second year at Hollantide in 1939 at 16/- per week, with full board and his insurance paid.

Robert Quirk, Lambfell, ploughing at the first Cronk-y-Voddy ploughing match held in a field alongside the 'Cronky' straight in 1938.

It was a time when the retail price of milk was 3d per pint, and the wholesale price of new potatoes began at 13/- per hundredweight in June, but soon dropped by September to 5s. and stayed there throughout the winter.

The Manx Government took control of meat marketing at the outbreak of war. All cattle, sheep and pigs ready for slaughter had to be sent to one of the three weekly marts. Beef cattle were paid for live weight at three grades: C, the best at £2.10s.6d. per hundredweight, CC at £2.10s. and CCC at £2.5s.

Fat lambs were sold on dressed carcase weight at 1/- per pound for top grade, dropping to 11d for grade three. We reared two pigs at a time for pork and bacon, feeding them on unsaleable potatoes and household scraps. The pigs had to be surrendered alive to the government who allowed us to buy (yes, buy back your own!) half a pig for the barrel – that is, salting the bacon for future use.

One way a farmer could balance his books and stay afloat in a sea of bankruptcies was to exploit his family and save on the wages bill. Billy Kelly may not have been overpaid, but I was worse off. Like most farm family members I was expected to work for half-a-crown a week pocket money on top of being clothed and fed. One memorable Saturday night on Douglas Promenade I pulled a handkerchief out of my pocket, and with it came my weekly 2/6d. in half-crown form. It rolled along the gutter and down a drain. Henry Taggart of Glencrutchery Farm, opposite the TT Grandstand, was with me and watched the coin disappear.

'That's all I've got!' I exclaimed. 'Sorry,' said Henry, 'I can't help you. I haven't got that much left.' Luckily I had the return half of the bus ticket and took an early bus home. I had no other option.

On January 2nd 1940, I recorded the stock on our 100 acres. There were seven working horses, 12 cows, a Shorthorn bull called Broadcaster, 32 young cattle, 47 breeding ewes and a Suffolk ram, three turkey hens and a stag, six ducks and an Aylesbury drake.

In addition to our own seven horses we also had on winter grazing three horses from tradesmen in Douglas. Two came from Herbert Kelly, carter and town cow keeper, the third from Daniel Shimmin & Son, baker and confectioner. The owners paid 1/6d per week for each horse's keep, which included us supplying hay when needed. The horses on keep lived outdoors, but our own were stabled from October to April.

The year 1940 marked a time when horse transport on the roads was being overtaken by the motor. The tradesmen's horses had been pensioned off but, as it happened, this proved premature. Wartime petrol rationing was soon introduced and by July 1942 the ration was severely reduced. For our old Morris Oxford car, which doubled as a van, we received just 21 gallons of petrol for the next three months. Not only the town tradesmen but we farmers, too, had to return to horses and carts.

Few farmers even dreamed that tractors would eventually replace horses for field work; horses would always be wanted, they thought, even if a tractor took over the heavier jobs. On April 10th 1942, my uncle bought a new horse plough. 'We'll always need it even if we do get a tractor, but I can't see we'll ever need one,' he said at the time. Incidentally, when we did acquire our first tractor in 1943 he was among the first farmers to look for ways of adapting horse implements to tractor power.

A new plough he bought in 1942 was one of the last horse ploughs to come to the Isle of Man. It was a Sellar 'medium' steel bar model, bought from Corlett Sons & Cowley Limited for £14.12s.9d, and was working, pulled by Prince and Billy, on the day it was delivered.

In 1997 it would be salvaged from the undergrowth in our haggart and rebuilt by Harold Leece of Greeba and Jack Collinson of Crosby. It is now used by Manx National Heritage at Cregneash and in ploughing matches.

Another acquisition of the time was a Blackstone potato digger pulled by two horses. It spun out the potatoes from the ridge, although we still had to pick them off the ground. War-time shortages and a government subsidy of £10 per acre spurred us to grow more potatoes. With the available labour, we managed to prepare the ground and plant five acres in spring, but harvesting them proved too much for my uncle and me. We were still graiping (forking) them out of the ridge by hand although sometimes we used a ridging plough to split the ridge and turn up the potatoes, although not without damaging many.

Bill Corteen was the last farmer in the Isle of Man to depend entirely on horses for field work. He is driving these three horses in an Albion binder at his farm, Thalloo Queen, at the Dhoon in Maughold in 1953.

Few attempts had been made to mechanise the shearing of sheep. Nevertheless on May 10th, 1940, we bought a new Lister sheep-shearing machine at a price of £5.4s, again from Corlett Sons & Cowley. But it was far from the labour-saver today's machines driven by electricity or small engine are. It required two men to operate it; one to turn a handle to drive the mechanism, another to shear the sheep. We discovered it was little faster than two men clipping with *joushes* (hand shears) but admittedly it was easier.

War brought another shock in the realisation that we had to grow on the farm almost all the food for our own livestock. Imported protein became so scarce that we were restricted to two bags of cake per month. We fed it just to the highest-yielding milking cows.

Neither agricultural society held summer shows during the two world wars. There were more important things to do, although the Isle of Man Agricultural Society still promoted its spring show with the encouragement of the government. It played a role in livestock breeding by encouraging the production of animals needed for food. The show was restricted to pedigree bulls and heavy horse stallions. On April 23rd 1942, in Ramsey, the best bull was shown by Alfred Christian, Ballacorey, Andreas, with the reserve from Ffinlo Corkhill, Ballagilley, Castletown. Both were Short-horns.

From the show we took delivery at Ballakilmartin of a black Aberdeen Angus named Magnet of Knockaloe. He was exhibited by Robert Moore of Port-e-Chee Farm, Braddan, from whom we bought him. Magnet was the last bull we ever had, because a great development in cattle breeding was soon to come along.

A demonstration was held at Ballafreer, Union Mills, farmed by Jim Looney, of the artificial insemination of a cow by the government vet Douglas Kerruish. In those days no woman ever attended the spring show because it was considered immodest for them even to look at bulls and stallions, rampant as many were. The women who turned up at Ballafreer were sent on a tour of the garden while the men witnessed an important development in cattle husbandry.

The first calf to be born in the Isle of Man by artificial insemination (AI) was a Friesian bull at Lower Sulby Farm, Onchan, for Robert G. Shimmin and his son Jack, on March 3rd 1943. Encouraged by this news, on June 2nd we had a dairy shorthorn cow, Rosebud, inseminated with semen from a shorthorn bull for which the Board of Agriculture had paid 300 guineas (£330) at an auction of the world-renowned Wreay herd in England. We paid 15/- as the insemination fee, but Rosebud did not take kindly to this unnatural form of mating and did not produce a calf.

'Serves you right for tampering with the higher order of things,' said the many critics of the technique. 'Even if the cow did have a calf it would probably have had two heads or five legs.'

But in our herd, as throughout the Isle of Man, AI was to prove highly successful. It enabled us to use the very best bulls we could never have afforded had we continued to buy our own.

This was just as well, because Magnet turned nasty and pinned my uncle against a wall a couple of times. Fortunately Aberdeen Angus cattle do not have horns and he escaped shocked, but without injury. My wife Laura also had a frightening experience when serving with the Women's Land Army in Ballaugh during the war. To this day she cites as grounds for divorce my acquiring of a bull!

Food supplies became desperately low, especially meat, which was needed not only for those at home but also for the armed services, many of whom were stationed on the Island. To encourage farmers to raise and fatten cattle for beef, on February 2nd 1940 the Manx Government decided to contribute 5/- per live hundredweight for beef animals when they were slaughtered. It was the start of the much-maligned subsidy system which many taxpayers considered was a free gift to inefficient farmers.

The 1940 legislation also fixed the price of meat in the shops, increasing beef by 2d. per pound. Perhaps it was after a hard and frustrating day on the farm that I wrote in my diary: 'It seems to me that the people who will profit most are the butchers, whose margin shoots up by one-and-half pence on every pound of beef they sell.'

On the other hand, working together in the community was one of the happier aspects of war and the years ahead were to see a concerted effort to win the conflict.

8
TRACTORS SUNK BY NAZI SUB

'There are still farmers using horses in England and Scotland, and they're needed for town work to pull drays and carts in Liverpool and Manchester', the flashily-dressed English horse dealer said when he called at our farm during the war.

We were gullible, perhaps because we wanted to believe him. After all I had reared Tom and George, two chestnut geldings, seeing them every day over the three years since they were born to our two mares which had the dual roles of working at the plough and breeding colts and fillies for future use.

Now we no longer needed these two as replacements since we acquired our first tractor in 1943. Nor

had my uncle and I the time to 'handle' them, first step in breaking them to chains or harness. Still, it was good to hear that there were people wanting young horses to work for the next 25 years, the average lifetime of a heavy horse.

I took fond farewells of my friends as I had done in the past with so many when they went on to other farms in the Island or in the UK. I petted them for the last time and assured them that they would be going to a good home. It was a few weeks later that the truth came – that they were shipped to England for slaughter as horse meat, to replace the beef so scarce throughout Britain.

Some of the meat returned here to supplement our own meagre rations. I discovered this later, when studying records classified as top secret in the war. Only the most heartening news was released at the time, in an effort to keep up morale.

Had I written this reference to horse meat then, it would have been deleted by the censor with a blue pencil to prevent publication. The slaughter of horses for meat was inevitable in the desperate situation in 1943, when the German U boats almost achieved their aim to starve Britain and the Isle of Man by sinking the food-carrying ships of the Merchant Navy. The

In double harness. Laura, driving the Nuffield tractor, and me setting off in September, 1953 to cut a field of oats, always known as corn in the Isle of Man.

Robert Callow, now of Ballig Farm, Onchan, ploughing with Clydedales in the Marown Royal Ploughing Match at Crosby in the 1950s.

coming of mechanisation left thousands of horses throughout Britain no longer wanted, and eating valuable feeding stuffs needed for other animals.

Horse meat was still helping to fulfil the weekly ration as late as 1949, and there was an outcry in Douglas Town Council when it was revealed that horses were being slaughtered at the town abattoir in Lake Road. 'I am sure we are all disgusted with the exhibition seen in the past week', complained Alderman J.H. Skillicorn.

But it was explained that the horses were being killed by authorisation of the Manx Government and the Corporation was powerless to prevent the practice. An assurance was given that the horse meat would not be eaten on the Island, but this proved untrue.

The Manx Government realised that if the Island was to produce the food it was capable of, from its fertile soil, faster, more efficient preparation of the land and harvesting of the crops were essential. It announced a scheme whereby a farmer could buy a tractor on credit terms. Grants, repayable in time, were made available, but so many farmers among 1,200 on the Island applied that the supply of tractors was far exceeded by demand.

At Ballakilmartin we had previously hired John Gorry of Middle Begoade, or the Board of Agriculture with their tractors, for heavy tasks such as ploughing or cutting corn. But we knew it would be much better to have a tractor of our own. In October 1942 my uncle took the big decision to order a new Fordson Red Spot at a cost of £170 from E. B. Christian & Co.. of Douglas. Rubber tyres were no longer available for farm tractors, so it would be fitted with steel wheels. Hopes of receiving it quickly were dashed, however, when we were told that 10 made in the USA and destined for the Isle of Man had been aboard a ship torpedoed and lost in the north Atlantic.

With this setback came news that no new tractors would be available because of the urgency to make planes and munitions.

But suddenly, on March 4th 1943, E.B. himself from E.B. Christian drove onto our farm street with a brand new Fordson – on steel wheels, but not yet fitted with the spade lugs for field work. It was a good job he did

Forty years after the launch of the Eastern Young Farmers' Club at Baldrine in 1943, founder members celebrated the anniversary at a dinner in the Castle Mona Hotel, Douglas in 1983. Pictured are (with married names of the ladies), front row: Barbara Kelly, Winnie Kneale, Kitty Quine, Armistice Quayle, Helen Moore. Second row: Nancy Taggart, Bob Dobson. Third row: John Moore, Jim Quilleash, John Clague, Mona Moore, Albert Moore. Back row: Ernest Kelly, Alec Kelly, Laurie Kelly, Harvey Briggs, Maurice Quine and Ewan Callow.

Erica Curphey, from Ballagyr, Peel (nee Erica Christian), leader of the Manx Women's Land Army, in full walking-out uniform and holding a prize-winning Aberdeen Angus bull belonging to Bertie Gill, Ballavarry, Andreas, at the Spring Show in Ramsey in 1943. With the coming of the Manx Women's Land Army two years earlier, the prejudice against women parading male sires, such a bulls and stallions, began to disappear.

Made by Ford in Michigan, our tractor came under the wartime lease-lend agreement between Britain and the USA. We had to get used to the petrol tank being labelled gasoline and the paraffin tank kerosene. It started on petrol and after five minutes warming up was switched to the cheaper paraffin or tractor vapourising oil. An allocation of 40 gallons of paraffin was issued by the Petroleum Board, but this did not last long with a fuel-guzzling Fordson.

I asked E.B. why he had chalked 'Hot' on the vertical exhaust pipe. 'Because,' he replied, 'I am tired of men used only to horses complaining that they have burned their hands on it!'

But the tractor was incomplete without a plough, and we had to wait until November 4th, eight months later, before we took delivery of a Massey Harris two furrow plough at a cost of £49. It was the type which trailed behind the tractor; few tractors were then fitted with hydraulic lift and three point linkage for attachment to implements.

The tractor age had dawned on our farm, but we still continued using horses until our last Clydesdale mare, Blossom, died in 1964. Nor did the tractor bring the luxury we expected. We rode rather than walked in the

not mention the price to my uncle, or he might well have had to drive it back to Douglas; when the bill came it had gone up to £190 – a ridiculous figure, my uncle complained.

Two days later George Corrin, a mechanic with the company, fitted spade lugs (without which the tractor could not move in soil) onto the wheels. And before he left the farm, George gave me my first lesson in tractor driving.

fields, but we spent many bitter winter days suffering on a machine open to the elements. We discovered when it rained why Ford had punched so many large holes in the driver's seat. A big overcoat stayed with the tractor, whoever the driver was. Today's waterproofs were unknown, and in any case we did not have the coupons required to purchase clothes either for work or best.

Tractors could replace horses but there was still a need for workers, especially as land that had lain derelict during the farming depression of the 1930s was now being cultivated again. Indeed it was said that with the coming of tractors, the horse had dropped out of the old adage 'Only fools and horses work. Now only the fools are left.'

On May 12th 1941, 'Spectator' wrote in his column in the *Isle of Man Examiner* that women should volunteer for work in the fields. He appealed to them: 'A great deal of important farm work can be done by women and as a large number of men have their evenings occupied with defence duties perhaps the women folk will come forward to help their native island as a matter of urgency.' He suggested that an odd evening or two working in the open air would have no more harmful effect than a visit to a local dance or the pictures.

A month later, on June 4th, the Manx Government launched the Manx Women's Land Army. Applicants would be trained at Knockaloe Experimental Farm for six to eight weeks, learning such skills as milking cows by hand, and would receive 30/- a week to pay for their board and lodging in nearby houses. When trained the girls would be placed to live on farms, or would join mobile squads based at Knockaloe or Lezayre Lodge near Sulby.

The initial response was poor; only 11 girls applied. Further appeals by George Howie, agricultural organiser, attracted a few more, and by March 1943 there were 43, of whom 23 lived on farms and 20 staffed the mobile squads. In all 89 girls were trained at Knockaloe, but others took up jobs on farms on their own initiative.

By 1945 there were 253 women (excluding farmers' wives) working on Manx farms although only 78 were actually WLA members. They were a valuable part of the 1,506 total work force (not including the farmers and their wives) engaged in agriculture.

On May 28th 1943, Manx people were to see something almost as unusual as women wearing trousers – women shearing sheep. They were competing in a Central Young Farmers' Club contest at Crosby. Shearing by hand (with *joushes*, the Manx name for shears) they had their own class, which was won by Millie Robinson (later a star racing cyclist) with her sister, Mabel, second, and Peggy Prescott third.

Other prizewinners were Belle Quayle, D. Tweeddale and J. Quayle, all WLA members. The women were allowed 45 minutes to shear a sheep against 25 for the men. Little did anyone expect that by the 1990s women would regularly surpass men in their sheep-shearing abilities!

Another source of labour for those farming near the camps were civilian internees and prisoners of war. They were allowed out to farms under guard or, once they could be trusted, on parole, picked up each morning at the camp gates and returned in late afternoon. We employed Italian aliens and German prisoners of war from the Onchan and Metropole camps. So desperate was the food situation in 1943 that the Italians were allowed out until 8pm in the fight to save the harvest.

A farmer paid 1/- per day to each man, plus 1/- weekly for insurance and as a contribution towards clothing. The internees were well fed on the farms and the comparative freedom they enjoyed meant that there were no shortages of volunteers.

The Young Farmers' movement had started in 1934 with the founding of the first Manx club, the Northern in Ramsey in January, followed by Central at Crosby in May. During the war they played an increasingly important role by helping to spread the gospel of good farming and promote methods of increasing vital food production.

Some of us from other districts occasionally travelled to the Northern and Central clubs without becoming regular attenders. When a joint meeting of the two clubs was held on a summer's evening at Glenlough Farm, Union Mills, to see how Tom Quayle and his sons, Henry and George, were building up a noted dairy herd, three young men cycled there from Onchan. We were Henry Taggart, Glencrutchery Farm, Bert Corkill from Corkill's Garage, and myself from Ballakilmartin.

During the course of the evening we were asked by the Central secretary, Annie Kneen of Peel, to join the club. 'It's all right now in the middle of summer but it's too far to travel on a bike in winter,' we replied. 'In that case,' said Miss Kneen, 'you need your own club'. She whisked us off to George Howie and announced that that was what we wanted.

A few weeks later Mr. Howie, in his uniform as a lieutenant colonel in the Home Guard and on his way to an exercise, stopped off at Baldrine to explain to a group of 19 young men and women the workings of a YFC, and so the Eastern club was launched.

John Clague, who had run the family farm of Ballavarane since the early death of his father, was elected the first chairman, Laurie Kelly, Bibaloe Beg, Onchan, later to become president of the Manx National Farmers' Union, vice chairman, and Jim Quilleash, Ballaragh, Lonan, who in the future was to be chairman of the Agricultural Marketing Society and of its Milk Marketing Association and Captain of the Parish of Lonan, treasurer. I, a shy young lad in

King George VI and Queen Elizabeth review the Manx Women's Land Army at Knockaloe Experimental Farm, Patrick on July 4th 1945. The King is talking to Erica Christian, (now Erica Curphey of Ballagyr, Peel) leader of the Manx Land Girls.

the back row, was plucked to the front to become secretary.

Whatever else I gained from the club, and there was much, it started me off writing on farming affairs for newspapers and journals at home and abroad. During four years as Eastern secretary and 10 as secretary of the YFC Federation, I sent in press reports to the four Manx newspapers, *Isle of Man Examiner*, *Isle of Man Times*, *Mona's Herald* and *Ramsey Courier*. When I gave up as federation secretary in 1957, I was invited by three of the editors to continue writing on general farming affairs.

While I was reporting for them, the *Isle of Man Times*, the *Mona's Herald*, the *Manx Star* and the *Ramsey Courier* all ceased publication! But happily, the *Isle of Man Examiner* still survives.

9
HARVEST CHANGED FOR EVER

I had hardly dropped off to sleep after a hard day's work on the farm when I was awakened by my aunt. 'Didn't you hear the siren?' she called. 'No'. 'Well it's gone off!'

I dressed hurriedly, donning my Civil Defence boiler suit, picked up my tin hat and gas mask, crossed the farmyard to mount my bicycle and pedalled like mad towards Onchan, negotiating the road block on the Whitebridge Hill designed to hamper invading troops. I reached the village, then only spreading sporadically into the countryside, and reported to police sergeant Fred Faragher at the ambulance post in Kelvin Road, known now as Monty's Lane because Monty Fargher's newsagent and hairdressing shop stood at the top.

It was 1942 and I was a member of the ARP (Air Raid Precautions) service, later to be renamed Civil Defence, which would come to the aid of the residents if bombs were dropped on Onchan.

The men with the guns were in the Home Guard, trained to capture the enemy in the event of an invasion following the fall of Dunkirk in May, 1940. The Isle of Man would never fall to Germany; we would defend our beloved Island with our lives if necessary. Those of us at home had a duty to protect our homeland while other young men and women went off to fight the foe.

As a member of the ambulance service I had to turn out at every air raid alert. There were around 30 of us in the Onchan First Aid section, and we were trained to handle casualties and convey them in an Onchan Laundry van to the clearing station in the basement of the Avenue Cinema, near the top of Royal Avenue.

Most of the lads were in the Home Guard – 'Dad's Army' to television viewers a generation later – but some near the centres of population enrolled as air raid wardens, firemen and ambulance men and women. For both the Civil Defence and the Home Guard there came a time when we were worn out through lack of sleep.

Practically every night the sirens sounded, and of course we had no rest during the day. The strain must have become apparent to those in command, because it was decided to draw up a rota whereby we had to turn out only on alternate alerts. Only a few stray bombs actually landed on the Island, dropped mainly by German planes missing their targets and jettisoning their loads in order to fly home faster and elude the RAF fighters.

Back on the farm we struggled to grow the food the people needed, not always successfully. Growing wheat for bread, 'the staff of life', was a disaster in 1943 and 1944. Each farmer had been ordered to allocate some of his land to wheat, but without suitable fertilisers yields were poor. Only a limited supply of superphosphate and sulphate of ammonia was allocated to each farm, depending on its acreage.

43

We grew, by order, 10 acres of wheat which in 1944 returned no more than 13 cwt per acre. A subsidy of £4 per acre just about covered the loss on the crop. In 1945 compulsory production of wheat was dropped, but the subsidy remained. It was not enough to attract many growers and only in recent years with the use of new technology has wheat become profitable and suitable for milling on around 20 of the Island's most fertile farms.

Oats were the main cereal on Manx farms, with 15,000 acres grown annually throughout the war years. Now there are fewer than 1,000 acres as the demand for oats for feeding working horses has almost disappeared and farmers find barley better for cattle and sheep. Fewer oats are needed for porridge, too, now that most people prefer cereals out of packets for breakfast.

Almost 18,000 acres of oats, wheat or barley were all gathered by the sheaf-and-stook method of harvesting, whereby the crop was cut and made into sheaves by a binder pulled by three horses or, increasingly, by tractors. The sheaves were left in the field for three weeks to mature before they were carted to stacks or dutch barns in the haggart. There, during the winter, they were threshed by a travelling mill with around 15 men from neighbouring farms gathering on one farm on a mill day.

For the 1944 harvest the first combine harvesters, which cut the crop and threshed it in one operation arrived in the Island. 'They'll never do here,' prophesied the critics. 'They are made for the American prairies, not our small fields and narrow lanes.' But two pioneering families were determined to prove otherwise.

Brothers Harry and Tyson Burrows, noted breeders of Hereford cattle and large grain growers at White House Farm, Kirk Michael, and John Clelland and his son Jack, early enthusiasts for British Friesian dairy cattle and ploughing broad acres at Lanjaghan in Abbeylands, Onchan, brought the first combines into the Island in the same shipment. They were identical models, Massey Harris trailer combines with Massey Harris pick-up balers.

At the White House combine and baler were hitched in tandem, pulled by an Allis Chalmers crawler tractor to complete the harvesting of the grain and the baling of the straw in one operation. At Lanjaghan the combining was done first with the use of a Cletrac crawler tractor and the straw was baled later.

The balers were a version of stationary balers adapted to pick up straw from the swathe. They needed two operators, one on each side of the bale chamber, both sitting on a bench and feeding into the needles the wire which bound the bales. They had to work fast to tie the wires before the bale was disgorged onto the ground. Modern balers bind and tie the bales automatically with twine and need no operators but the tractor driver.

Excitement ran high, and crowds flocked to both farms to see these wonderful contraptions in action. They travelled miles on foot or on bicycle, because petrol was severely rationed. At Lanjaghan the Clelland family cashed in by collecting money for the Red Cross.

The speed of mechanisation in Manx agriculture is reflected in the arrival of a machine which could do the work of 10 or a dozen men and women reaping by scythe or sickle not many years before. Only a short distance away from Lanjaghan at Ballacoyne the last oxen pulled a plough in a Manx field in 1912, just 32 years before the coming of the combine.

Robbie Quirk – Kirk, his neighbours called him – used a heifer and a horse in harness, the last known relic of ploughing with oxen.

'I think nothin' of them new-fangled English ideas. The oul' ways are the best.' Fortunately for the survival of Loaghtan sheep, the last native breed of livestock apart from the Island's suspect cats, Robbie stuck with them, resolutely refusing to introduce improved British breeds to his flock. His Loaghtans were the ancestors of many of those now remaining.

September 1944 saw the first combine harvester appear on the Island at Lanjaghan, Onchan. It created a lot of interest and one of the first parties to visit the equipment was the Eastern Young Farmers Club. The outfit is seen here with Jack Clelland driving the Cletrac tractor and Herbert Cain on the Massey Harris combine.

'At a special ram sale at Ramsey we buy a Kerry Hill ram lamb for £5. This ram, bred by Joseph Callister, Ballavitchel, Crosby, will run with the flock in addition to our older Dorset Horn ram.

'At the ram sales prices for well-bred rams reached double figures, probably for the first time, but inferior quality animals are harder to sell. Farmers are realising that only the best rams will beget the quality of lamb necessary to obtain top grades. Fat lamb production is more remunerative now than at any time since the 1914-18 war. The reasons are the same, the scarcity of sheep under wartime conditions.'

A significant feature in Manx cattle farming is that the total number of milking cows has remained static over the years. The figure of 7,583 60 years ago is almost the same as the 7,784 today. But better breeding and management have pushed up yields to around three times their previous peak in 1945. At the same time the 420 farmers' milking cows then have dropped to 81 in 2001.

In a drastic twist the average number of cows in a Manx herd has risen from 18 in 1946 to 97 in 2001. With this, too, has come a complete swing from milking by hand to milking by machine.

Throughout the war there remained a serious shortage of labour in agriculture. On November 17th 1944 there was an appeal in the Manx newspapers for volunteer potato-pickers to secure the crop before winter closed in. On our own farm we still had two acres in the ground, and with the Italian internees in the Onchan and Metropole camps being moved to Ramsey, there was nowhere left to turn for help.

Food rationing continued and rations still stood at weekly allowances of three ounces each of butter and bacon, two of cheese and tea, eight of sugar and four

In my youth in Braddan I met people who remembered Robbie sowing oats and barley out of an old top hat, long discarded by some gentleman for best wear.

In 1943 the sheep population of the Isle of Man stood at 75,000, compared with 178,000 today. They were not encouraged during the war because they were accused of eating grass needed for cattle, which could provide the much needed protein for humans in the form of meat or milk. Besides, the grass sheep grazed was being ploughed up to grow grain now that hardly any could be imported.

The great improvement in grass for pasture, hay or silage was not to come until after the war, through experiments in Wales by Sir George Stapledon. Nevertheless each farmer in the Island's mixed farming system endeavoured to hold onto his flock. Here is my own experience, described on August 6th, 1943:

During the worrying times of World War II, the efforts being made by the Onchan War Agricultural Committee were boosted by a visit to the Island of Earl and Lady Granville here pictured front centre at Government House.

of sweets and chocolate. We were encouraged to make the most of what we had. Lord Woolton, the UK Minister of Food, told us: 'Apple cores can be turned into delicious and very health-giving drinks by boiling them in water.'

In the UK people were restricted to one egg per person per week. There was no egg rationing in the Isle of Man, but they became very scarce, and there were frequent calls to our farm by people looking for half a dozen or even less. One woman pleaded regularly: 'My husband has to keep his strength up for his work and I am relying on you and our long friendship to help.'

Meat was a little more plentiful in the Island, the ration standing at 1/3d. worth here when it was just 8d. worth per week in the UK. The Isle of Man's close proximity to the neutral Republic of Ireland was a great help, but the less said about that the better . . .

When the Italian internees we employed were released in 1944 they gave me their working clothes. These were very useful, because I had long since spent my meagre supply of coupons.

46

10

A CHILLY AFFAIR

'Will the farmers' horses go?' asked a headline in the *Isle of Man Times* on January 14th, 1939. Well they did, because at the time there were 3,770 working horses and now there are none used regularly in the Island except by Manx National Heritage at Cregneash.

In 1939 there were fewer than 40 tractors on Manx farms. But by 1950 tractor numbers had grown to over 1,000, while the heavy horse population dropped steadily until in 1979 it was recorded by the Board of Agriculture at a mere 15. Today, due to determined efforts by breeders to save the magnificent Clydesdales and Shires from extinction, there are around 100 of them in the Island.

In 1939 the *Isle of Man Times* was reporting on what it described as the first mechanical ploughing match. Six tractors – no horses – took part in a demonstration and competition at the government's experimental farm at Knockaloe.

'This was the strangest ploughing match the Isle of Man has ever seen,' wrote the reporter. 'There were no sturdy, groomed and be-ribboned teams of horses, and the picture of a fine pair followed by plough and man and hosts of screaming gulls was replaced by overalled figures on the seats of machines driven steadily up and down with exhausts spluttering and turning over the land at a speed which made the older methods look slow and laborious.'

Another difference was that each tractor had to plough three-and-a-half acres of land, rather than the few furrows more common at traditional matches.

In addition to prizes for the best ploughing there were awards for the lowest fuel consumption. Judges William Radcliffe from Ballalheaney, Andreas, and Percy Kermode, Creggans Farm, Castletown, gave first prize to E.B. Christian & Co., with an entry of a Fordson tractor and Sellar plough. Quayle's Garage took second and third prizes with Ferguson tractors, one petrol driven, the other by vapourising oil, both with Ferguson ploughs. Fourth were Corlett Sons & Cowley Ltd. putting to work a Bristol Caterpillar tractor and Lister plough.

Despite the invention of rotary cultivators which prepare ground for crops in one operation, ploughing has remained over the years the most widely used form of cultivation, provided it is done properly.

The first Manx match had been held in 1840 at Ballavargher at the Cooil, Braddan, with teams of both horses and oxen pulling the ploughs. It was a pouring wet day and only eight out of the 13 teams entered turned up. By the next year 23 teams ploughed in Port-e-Chee Meadow near Douglas, and they were a magnificent sight with even the oxen decorated with ribbons.

Until the tractor trial at Knockaloe in 1939 only horses and, further back in history, cattle pulled ploughs. The first match with horses and tractors was held on our farm of Ballakilmartin on January 31st, 1946. A sunny morning gave way to torrential rain in

Left: John Lace from Maughold ploughs a neat furrow at the Mannin Ploughing Match at Ballamona Hospital farm, Braddan. Right: Willie Caine, with measuring stick, checks the size of furrows watched by his son, Norman, crouching, and Donald Cannan, holding the horses. They are on their home ground of Cronk-y-Voddy.

the afternoon. Eleven tractors and four pairs of horses competed, indicating the swing to mechanical power during the war years.

It was the first post-war match although the Cronk-y-Voddy match, like the Windmill Theatre in London, never closed; it was held each year from 1940 to 1945. Indeed, the story is told that when in 1946 someone asked the Cronky lads if they knew the war was over, they said they did: 'But tell us, what happened to the Kaiser?'

Although I was living at Ballakilmartin in 1946 I saw little of the match, which attracted spectators and competitors from all over the Island. The tractors made channels which sent the downpour of rain cascading into the

back of the farm house. I and a friend, Fletcher Craine, were kept busy baling out water from the kitchen before it could reach the front room – where the new Lieutenant Governor, Sir Geoffrey Bromet, was being entertained by the committee of the Lonan and Onchan Ploughing Society and the chairman of the Board of Agriculture and MHK for Middle, Harry Cowin.

They were no doubt discussing, like everyone at the match, the merits of horses and tractors for farm work. 'I'll stick to my horses,' declared one prominent farmer. 'I can feed them with what I grow on the farm so I don't have to buy fuel. And they don't cut up the fields like tractors.'

Jack Shimmin, then of Lower Sulby Farm, Onchan, helps his son-in-law Marshall Corlett set the plough for competition work.

'Rubbish,' retorted his friend. 'The tractor eats nothing when it's not working and I've got all the power I need for the heavier work.'

We know now who won the argument, although anyone bold enough to suggest in those days that tractors would completely replace horses would have been labelled insane.

During the war the Parish War Agricultural Committees, comprising about a dozen worthy farmers in each parish, appointed by the government, had developed a dual role. In addition to policing the production of food on each farm, indeed each field, they were instigators of fund-raising appeals for war charities.

In Onchan the committee organised an auction of animals and produce at Government House with the governor, Earl Granville, and his wife, Lady Rose – sister of the Queen Mother – as hosts. They welcomed visitors to their home for whist drives and attended concerts in the Avenue Cinema in Onchan.

Top prize at a whist drive and dance held in the Villa Marina on January 29th 1943 was a repeater chiming watch complete with heavy gold chain, valued at 40 guineas (£42) pre-war. Onchan Farmers War Effort announced that it had been provided by an anonymous donor. I still have the ticket which cost me 1/6d. and gave me admission to the Villa. Who won the watch, and is it still around? It would be hard to estimate its value today.

The war ended with VE Day (Victory in Europe) on May 8th, 1945, although we had to wait until August 15th for VJ Day (Victory in Japan). I celebrated VE Day in two contrasting ways: first at a special service of thanksgiving in St. Peter's Church, Onchan, then by cycling to Laxey to join a huge crowd at a dance in the Workingmen's Institute.

At midnight the air raid siren at Laxey police station sounded the all clear to mark the official end of the European war. Recording it at the time, I wrote: 'Next day, organised at short notice, a Victory Parade is held in Onchan. I play my part by leading our horse, Billy, pulling a farm lorry through the village to an afternoon of sports and revelry in a field on Groudle Road.

'On board the lorry are members of Onchan Young People's Fellowship, dressed to represent our war heroes. In the evening there is more dancing in the village hall to the music of a Royal Marines Band. 'There'll Always Be An England' has a special significance. Somewhere in between I find the time and energy to help the milking by hand of our 15 cows. Thankfully there is little other work on the farm because in May all the cattle and sheep are getting their living at grass and the arable work is at a standstill for a few days in the epoch-making period in history.'

The War Agricultural Committees and the

Agricultural Marketing Society had administrative roles in farming affairs, both having been set up under Tynwald legislation. The Isle of Man Farmers' Club, founded in 1865, and the two agricultural societies, the Isle of Man (later Royal Manx) dating from 1858 and the Southern, born in 1914, were important in their own specialised activities. Only 'the club' had a political influence in addition to its co-operative trading on behalf of members and was usually consulted by the government or anyone wanting to hear the views of

Lonan and Laxey ploughing match around 1936. The event was held at Baldrine Farm, the home of Mr J. Tom Clucas, at the top of Baldrine Hill. Pictured, front row, left to right, are: Edward Christian, Kirby Farm, Braddan, judge; John Cottier, Baldromma Moar, Lonan, secretary; Robert C. Quayle Ballacreggan, Port Soderick, judge; Tom Caveen, Shonest, Lonan, chairman; Walter Cowin, MHK and Mrs Cowin; Alfred Chrystal, Ramsey, horse judge; Wilfred Callow, Port-e-Chee, Braddan, judge; Jacob Lewin, Ballacarrooin, Braddan. Back row, left to right: Charlie Condra, Baldromma, Lonan; Harry Bridson, Ballacojeen, Lonan; Robert Kelly, Rhaa Farm, Lonan; Stanley Kerruish, Onchan; Herbert Corlett, Ballabeg.

50

farmers. But there was a feeling among farmers that it was not fully representative of the industry, because not all farmers belonged to it and as a trading company it was not always fully independent in its views.

The War Agricultural Committees had proved their worth in encouraging farmers to work together, and Deemster Ramsey Johnson suggested in 1946 that with their duties over they could be the basis of an organisation to speak for the whole industry.

A meeting was called for a Saturday afternoon in October 1946 at St. Matthew's Hall, Douglas. Believe it or not, I was ejected from the meeting although I have since lived to become one of four life members of the Manx National Farmers' Union formed that day - the others are Ian Anderson, Peter Kennaugh, both past presidents and Noel Cringle, President of Tynwald.

The reason for my exclusion centred around a screen of secrecy about the founding of a union. There was a strong town-versus-country divide in Tynwald, and often the farmers' cause was hampered by dissent among the rural members themselves.

'A farmer's worst enemy is another farmer' was a saying that could be confirmed by anyone who ever tried to sell potatoes, vegetables, eggs and milk around the streets of Douglas. In times of plenty there was so much price undercutting that there was no margin for profit in production.

But 'Unity is strength' was the slogan for the founding fathers of the Farmers' Union. 'Try to break one stick, it's easy. Put a bunch together and you'll never do it,' echoed their policy.

Each war committee member was invited to attend the inaugural meeting and instructed to bring the invitation card bearing their name and address. My uncle could not go and, knowing my growing interest in farming politics, he passed on his invitation card to me. I wandered unchallenged into the hall and was sitting down when an officious steward swooped, checking that everyone had a card. I showed him mine and he responded: 'You are not James McCubbin. I know him. You can't stay here. Please get out.'

I was walking dejectedly along North Quay when I met Billy Moore of Begoade Farm, a neighbour. 'Aren't you going to the meeting?' he asked. I explained what had happened. 'Come with me. If this union is not going to encourage young people it's got no future.' So I sat there sheepishly among 80 others, not saying a word but watching another chapter of history in the making.

Ramsey Johnson and a handful of supporters visited every one of the 17 parishes in the following winter, which in the early months of 1947 brought the worst snow and frost in living memory. Shivering in cold halls, they preached the gospel of political change in agriculture and established in each parish a committee with a secretary, headed by a chairman who would have a seat on the all-Island council.

The year 1946 also saw the formation of a fourth Young Farmers' Club to complete coverage throughout the Isle of Man. The Southern club was formed on February 20th in Arbory Parish Hall.

With four clubs it was logical to bind them together into a federation, which was immediately recognised for its influence among the young people of the countryside and was frequently invited to express its views at government level, not least to the various commissions appointed to look at rural life.

With the founding of the Manx NFU and the Isle of Man Federation of YFCs, no longer could the opponents of farming accuse it of being a divided, self-destructing industry.

11
GERMAN TROOPS ON OUR FARM

I tasted ice cream for the first time in five years on April 26th 1945. It was at the official stand-down of Onchan Civil Defence held in the Howstrake Hotel (now Molly's Kitchen).

Ice cream-making had been banned in 1940 so that all milk could be used for liquid consumption or for manufacture into cheese to keep up the meagre ration of two ounces per person per week. Imported cheese was no longer available.

We enjoyed a four-course dinner including roast turkey as the main course that day. Poultry was not rationed, unlike other meat. Until then hotels and restaurants were not allowed to serve more than two courses, and the price of the meal was not to exceed 5/-, which precluded the serving of any luxuries even if they had been available.

VE day was followed by VJ day on August 15th when I joined a large crowd dancing in the roadway on Douglas promenade to the music of Billy Ternent and his band, playing on the parapet above the Villa Marina arcade. With the end of war we expected life would return to normal, yet it was not until 1954 that some foods were sufficiently plentiful to allow the complete end of rationing.

On June 1st 1945, the petrol ration was increased to five gallons per month, and motorists were allowed to use their cars for pleasure instead of only in connection with business (which included farming). I wrote in my diary: 'On the face of it, the basic allowance of five gallons is not much of an inducement to pleasure motoring but as one local newspaper comments "a little basic goes a long way", a reference to the black market where almost anything can be bought at a price.'

On July 31st 1946, the mobile squads within the Manx Women's Land Army were disbanded and Lezayre Lodge, their hostel, was closed. Sixteen members still lived in and worked on individual farms.

But not for them a celebratory dinner, nor the gratuity, nor the suit or dress every other service person received on demobilisation. The land girls' uniforms were called in to be kept, presumably, for the next war. Are they lying in some government building to this day? One thing certain is that they are not at Knockaloe, the base for the WLA.

The Manx girls did receive a derisory issue of 10 clothing coupons, scant reward for up to five years of service. The WLA throughout Britain was accorded the same shabby treatment, resulting in the resignation of its head, Lady Denman, who went on to divert her organisational skills to the Women's Institute movement.

Farmers had been promised, when the food they produced was desperately needed to help win the war, that never again would their industry be neglected as it was in the 1930s. They would be given priority, and when enough food could be grown at home cheap imported supplies would be prohibited, a promise broken so many times that I no longer trust any politicians.

There were other issues besides agriculture to be considered in the post-war Isle of Man. We had all been subject to so much official control of our lives that we looked forward to the freedom President Roosevelt told us we were fighting for.

When one young serviceman returned to Onchan he stood for the House of Keys for the sheading of Middle, then comprising Onchan village and the parish of Onchan, Braddan and Santon. He was Jack Nivison, a native of Onchan, and he was a Labour Party candidate. Frustrated by his failure to procure a hall for the crucial eve of poll meeting, he mounted a soap box in Auburn Road ready to speak to anyone prepared to listen. Late on a sunny May evening he found his audience in the crowd that poured out of the village hall in Royal Avenue, which had been booked by the 'old guard', the three retiring members on the one platform.

Jack was being interrupted by a persistent heckler. Without losing his cool he called to the man, 'Do you believe in controls, sir?' 'Yes,'

Threshing at Kella Farm, Sulby in 1940, prior to the introduction of tractors. Crennell's Clayton and Shuttleworth engine is threshing for Percy Radcliffe and the sacks of oats are being loaded onto a motor lorry for sale off the farm.

(Photo: Stephen Carter)

At Caley's Booilshuggel farm in East Baldwin, R. G. Shimmin's Fowler compound traction engine driven by Walter Creer, working with threshing mill, circa 1935.

(Photo: Stephen Carter)

In 1946 a young Mr Charles Kerruish, farming at Ballafayle, Maughold, commenced a distinguished political career. He was always par-ticularly proud of his farming connections and he is seen here at a quiz held at Onchan Park Restaurant where the contesting sides were from the Eastern Young Farmers Club and the Onchan Branch of the Manx National Farmers' Union. Charles (later Sir Charles) is seen front left with His Honour Ramsey Johnson, MNFU President (centre) and Edward Brownsden, MHK for Middle on the right. Standing, left to right are: Paul Shimmin, Wilfred Callin, William E. Moore, Robert G, Shimmin, John Gelling, Henry Taggart, Ernest Kelly and the author.

came the reply. 'Then kindly control your mouth,' came Jack's rejoinder.

It was the stuff political meetings were made of in those days before television, when we looked to the local scene for a bit of excitement – although eggs were too scarce to be wasted on politicians.

Jack Nivison lost that election, but went on to win a by-election on October 18th 1948, succeeding Clifford Kniveton who had resigned. A crusading spokesman for agriculture and a product of the Northern Young Farmers' Club, Charles Kerruish from Ballafayle in Maughold began the distinguished political career which ended with his appointment as first President of Tynwald when he was elected to represent Garff at the 1946 general election.

Although most farmers had acquired a tractor, usually their first, during the war, horses still held pride of place on many farms and both were used in the fields. One of the disadvantages of tractors was that apart from ploughs there were few implements designed for them. Farmers and blacksmiths working together became adept at adapting horses' tackle for tractor draught. The degree of ingenuity established almost a trade in itself, examples being the fitting of corn binders with new hitches, and making bows to enable more kipps (sections) of harrows to be joined together. Local joiners built trailers with a larger capacity than horse carts and fitted with draw bars rather than shafts.

In the late 1940s and throughout the 1950s it seemed certain that horses would always be kept for lighter work, especially when more men to drive them became available on their return from the war. The early tractors were not always reliable and occasionally broke down.

On April 11th 1945, for instance, our Fordson, bought new two years previously, refused to start. Starting it was always hard work anyway, because it involved cranking the engine with a handle before electric starters were introduced. Tempers became frayed throughout the morning because the land was just right for preparing for oats. It was a couple of days later before a mechanic detected that the vapouriser was blocked with carbon.

A few weeks later it stopped again, in the middle of a crucial harvest, because of a faulty magneto and we had to wait almost a week for replacements. On another occasion it stood idle for days because the Manx Government's Petroleum Board had not enough delivery wagons to cope with all the orders, and tractor fuel could not be obtained elsewhere.

It was not surprising then, that some farmers refused to rely completely on tractors but inevitably most changed their minds; by the late 1960s hardly a working horse was left on a Manx farm.

Gradually, too, the hiring of men (and a few women) at Hollantide for a year's contract gave way to weekly or monthly terms of employment. But single men still depended on a job and a home on a farm. When a man changed farms he was often put to sleep with another man in a double bed. Years after, when two men sharing a bed would have led to all kind of rumours, I asked a man who had spent a lifetime on farms what his views were on the subject.

'I tell you this, boy, nothing ever happened,' he said. 'One false move and you'd have had a fist in your face.' Incidentally, the word 'gay' was used frequently on Manx farms in those days. It referred to a mare which was in season and ready to be mated to the travelling stallion.

The end of the steam era came suddenly, for a reason few could have foreseen. After the war the miners went on strike in the UK and coal became scarce in the Isle of Man. On our own farm we took delivery of almost four tons from a shipment imported by the Isle of Man Farmers' Club on December 23rd 1946, but that was to be the last in such quantity for a long time.

The steam engines which pulled and powered the threshing outfits consumed around half a ton a day and soon farmers, who provided the coal, were struggling to find enough for mill days. Luckily the noisy but powerful single cylinder diesel-driven Field Marshall tractors were being built by then, and they replaced the giant steam engines, most of which were dismantled for their scrap metal still in demand due to various shortages. So the urgent *putt, putt, putt* of the Field Marshall was heard rather than the more leisurely *puff, puff, puff* of the steam engine.

One welcome change was that no longer did the engine driver need to be on the farm at 6am to raise steam on the engine for an 8am start to threshing. The Field Marshall was started either by use of a cartridge in the engine or by cranking with a handle. It, together with the Nuffields and David Browns which were also used for threshing, could be made ready for work five minutes before they were needed.

Using tractors did not reduce the number of men required, and around 15 still gathered at each farm's mill day. The spread of combine harvesters after the first two came to the Island in 1944 was slow.

Four years on I recorded on September 16th 1948: 'Frank Kinnish is here cutting oats with a tractor and binder from the Board of Agriculture's contracting service. We take time off to cross the road to Bibaloe Moar to see Eddie Coole's new combine harvester put to work. It is the fourth to come to the Island. John Clelland at Lanjaghan, Onchan, and brothers Harry and Tyson Burrows had the first in 1944, followed by Jack Shimmin at Lower Sulby Farm in Onchan two years later. The latest is an International Harvester combine pulled by a wheeled tractor of the same make.'

Jack Shimmin's Massey Harris 222 was the first self-propelled combine to come to the Island, meaning that it had its own engine and did not need a tractor to pull it. Low slung, with small wheels, it gave problems when travelling over steeper and more uneven fields than it had been designed for in Canada where it was built.

In March 1945 we harvested four acres of potatoes which had been in the ground since the seed was planted exactly a year before. When it came to the usual lifting time in autumn we had no help, and when winter came on the weather was against us.

The Italians interned in the Onchan and Metropole camps were released or moved to Ramsey and there was no other source of labour until German prisoners of war came to the Manx camps. At the time farmers had to employ a gang of 12 prisoners and we agreed to those terms and borrowed a potato digger for use with a tractor from our neighbour at Begoade, Tommy Faragher. The result was that 12 Germans in Wehrmacht and Luftwaffe uniforms, flanked by two of their own officers and two British armed guards, marched through Onchan on the way to our farm.

The Germans had expected to walk on Manx soil as conquerors. They told me so, in halting English, but they were in good spirits, were glad to be alive and were looking forward to returning to their own homes. Like us they welcomed what both sides knew was the end of the war.

12
LOO WITH A LIGHT

There was great excitement on our farm one September day in 1945. Our new landlord, Councillor Stephen A. Quirk, Mayor of Douglas, told us that now the war was over we were to get a bathroom and inside toilet in our 400-year-old farmhouse. No longer would we have to stumble down the garden by the light of a candle, when it was dark and perilous enough in the daylight to the two-seater earth closet *thie veg*. During the blackout, which ended on September 7th 1944, we dared not show a light even when going to the lavatory.

I had never had a chance to share the delights of the two-seater side-by-side toilet, and indeed wondering about the need for it. Probably it was designed for a family with young children to train in its use. There were no such things as toilet rolls, and we used in their place square strips of newspaper. Sitting there in daylight was one way of catching up with any news we had missed.

At the same time the house was connected to the mains water supply running up the White Bridge Hill, instead of depending on springs on the farm. With the installation of a bath we now had the luxury of its regular use, rather than carrying hot water in a jug to an enamel dish in the bedroom for an occasional spongedown before we were fit to mix with civilised company.

Life on the farm was improving in many ways although we would have to wait until 1952 for a proper electricity supply.

We spent more time riding on a tractor seat and less plodding after horses, although we still retained three heavy horses and used them regularly. Gradually we got out of the habit of shouting 'Whoa!' when we wanted the tractor to stop.

We learned not to strike a match to look into the fuel tank of a tractor to see if it needed filling. One of my friends did that, and lived to tell the tale into ripe old age – but it would be unfair of me to name him because many of us made mistakes in the transition to farming with tractors.

We discovered that tractors had to be driven with care on steep *brooghs* (banks). Ploughing and harrowing could be accomplished with care because the implement could be used as an anchor in an emergency, but when the tractor was hitched to a field roller or wheeled vehicles like trailers or corn binders there were often some hairy moments. The result is that many *brooghs*, including two on our own farm, have not been cultivated since the end of the horse era.

We did not realise it but we were the pioneers, the adventurers, the inventors carving out a new chapter in the 2,000 years of Manx agricultural history. Working the fields was just one part of our daily lives. Most of the Island's 1,200 farms were mixed in the sense that any way they could produce food was utilised. 'The farmer produces everything we eat except fish, and everything we wear except jewellery,' we were told. 'Come what may you will always be needed', trumpeted our leaders, especially at election time when around half of the Keys' privileged 24 depended on the farming industry to elect them.

The mixed farm economy meant producing something of everything for the local market. Cows provided milk, beef and leather, sheep supplied meat and wool, and pigs were kept for their pork and bacon. Poultry gave us eggs and meat from chickens, turkeys, ducks and geese. In the fields we grew potatoes, vegetables and grain. Nothing was wasted, and in the event of a loss on one product we could generally survive on a profit from others. The family farm run on these lines was the backbone of a rural economy which supported, in full or in part, around 2,000 other tradesmen and ancillary workers throughout the Island.

The farmers used every square yard of land, ploughing the last furrow from each field and trimming the hedges back to their stone and sod structure. All this maintained the countryside in good heart and enhanced its appearance and appeal by keeping down undesirable growth such as weeds and encroaching gorse and brambles.

If all this has changed it is due to world conditions which declare that a country, including the Isle of Man, buys its food from wherever it is cheapest rather than allowing home farmers to have the first call on their local market. 'A nation should be fed from its own land,' was the cry before the European Union and the General Agreement on Trade and Tariffs decided they knew better.

During World War One vast fortunes were made by farmers who had the land and labour to grow scarce food. From 1939 the Manx Government determined that there should be no profiteering in this war. All farm products were controlled in price and distributed under government direction.

Auction of growing animals was still permitted, but prices automatically stayed at a level related to their fixed value as a finished product. The price of calves in the three marts, at Ramsey, Ballasalla and St.

John's, dropped to as low as 1/- each because of the scarcity of milk or replacement feed with which to rear them.

But calf prices did recover, and on April 30th 1945, I returned from Ramsey Mart with the news that a bull calf I had taken there fetched £2.15s. and a heifer £2.2s. Both were the progeny of our Aberdeen Angus bull, Magnet of Knockaloe, out of Shorthorn cows. On July 2nd two more calves, again a bull and a heifer, made £3 each. Life was definitely looking brighter.

A black yearling bullock weighing six hundredweight which we consigned to Ramsey Mart in April sold at £21, and on July 23rd we had another good day, selling two-year-old store cattle at £3.18s. per hundredweight and 10 fat lambs at the controlled price of 1/- per pound carcass weight.

The weeks following the end of the war saw several farm sales around Hollantide, most having been delayed until the end of hostilities. We bought a young cow for £16 at Ballamoar, on the Ramsey Road north of Laxey, where Lou Maddrell was giving up farming, and another at Camlork Farm, Mount Rule, Braddan, from Tom Cain at £26. Both cows were Shorthorns, which then comprised 90% of the national herd.

At Ballameanagh, near Baldrine, my uncle's bid of 15/- secured a grass seed drill mounted on a single-wheeled barrow and I brought it home next day by pony and float. Other auctions I attended as a day out without buying anything were at Castleward, Braddan, where Tom Kelly was moving out, and at Close Lake, Andreas, which at that time had one of the Island's airports and had been farmed by Willie Brew MHK.

Bibaloe Beg, near Onchan village, changed ownership and with the change came a temporary pause in at least two emerging features of Manx agriculture. Tom Kniveton and his sons, Norman and Clifford, had introduced the first complete herd of British Friesian cattle and they had made cereal silage to feed them on. Robert Kelly and his family continued both the pure Friesian herd and the silage during five years as tenants until 1944, but when Harry Moore of Brownwood bought Bibaloe he reverted to the more conventional Shorthorn cows and fed them on turnips and hay.

This proved a mere hiccup, however, in the onward march of Manx agriculture; today Holsteins – virtually another name for Friesians – are the principal dairy breed and silage is the most widely-used winter feed.

A talking point in 1945 was the sale of the Island's biggest lowland farm, the 650-acre Ellerslie at Crosby, to R. Gilbert Corlett, owner of Laxey Glen Mills, where most of the flour for the Island's bread was milled. Sellers were the Cunningham family, who ran Cunningham's Camp in Victoria Road, Douglas, a Mecca for young men at holiday time. The farm helped to feed them as well as supplying milk for retail rounds in Douglas.

Here is my comment at the time: 'It is not generally known what the purchase price is, but last year Harley Cunningham expected £16,000 for the show- place. The buildings undoubtedly are the finest of any farm on the Island and, according to the *Isle of Man Times* this week, among the best half-dozen in Britain. This may be true of the farm steading but the land is light and sandy overlying rock with little depth of soil and not at all the type of land termed good by agriculturalists.'

Mr Corlett took over following the auction of livestock and machinery on October 19th.

'No bargains today; the name Cunningham, Ellerslie, ensured that,' I wrote. 'I hurried home to do the yard work before setting off for Laxey, where in the Workingmen's Institute an RAF dance band from Jurby played to a packed gathering for the Eastern Young Farmers' Mhelliah.'

As president of the Eastern YFC, Gilbert Corlett took his duties seriously, and he turned up at the dance after the sale at the farm he had bought.

The spring show of breeding bulls and heavy

horse stallions continued throughout the war to encourage livestock breeding, but in 1945 there was only just time after peace was restored to organise the first summer agricultural show since 1939. In warm sunshine on Thursday, August 2nd, the summer show staged by the Isle of Man Agricultural Society was a chance for a joyful reunion of those who had survived a long war.

I reported: 'A record crowd gathered at the Nunnery park, with holidaymakers back in Douglas in huge numbers strolling out from the town to join residents from all over the Island. Entries of livestock are not as high in quantity or quality as pre-war and the trade stands have little to display.'

*Whilst Agricultural Shows at the Nunnery had resumed in 1946 after the war, 1951 saw the first **Royal** Manx Agricultural Show staged there. The seal of royal approval had just been awarded and the show drew a large crowd.*

'The women put on a grand feed in the catering tent, a welcome return to the hospitality countryfolk are noted for after so much austerity.'

Sixty years ago there was a lot of superstition in farming and the countryside. Because none of us fully understood the annual miracle which ensured that the seed we planted in spring matured into a source of food by autumn, we were inclined to heed the advice handed down by those who had tilled the same land before us.

One belief that survives to this day – because I, for one, still honour it – is never to start a big job on a Friday. I remember when one Thursday in March we had a field ready to plant in potatoes and intended beginning the next day, my uncle sent me with a spade and a dozen setts (seed potatoes) to plant them so that we did not start on a Friday.

Until 1940 no one ever worked in the fields on a Sunday, although the animals still had to be fed, watered, cleaned out and – for cows – milked. The Manx Government was partly blamed for breaking the Sabbath. It established a contracting service with tractors to help vital food production in wartime. The drivers were issued with a letter informing farmers that the outfit must work on a Sunday, and if a farmer refused to do so then the driver must continue to the next customer.

Soon we were all working on Sundays at busy seasons. Was it coincidence or had we invoked the wrath of someone higher up that we lost almost the entire hay harvest through incessant rain in 1942, the first year we had tried to make hay on a Sunday? There were many of an older generation who said that if we had not broken the Sabbath the crop would have been saved.

13

THE SHEEP UNDER THE SNOW

The weather has a profound effect on farming and in over 70 years spent on two Manx farms, first in Braddan, then in Onchan, two prolonged spells stand uppermost in my mind. Arctic conditions in the early months of 1947 meant weeks when the land was covered in snow and the temperature rarely rose above freezing. In 1954, the promise that seed-time and harvest will never fail came close to being broken during months of incessant rain.

Everything else about the weather reflects a stability sufficient to support a farming system which, if left to the men and women who work the land, could supply most of the needs of its inhabitants and still leave food for export to the benefit of the economy. There were even those with great Christian faith who claimed that God was on the side of the righteous during two world wars in sending suitable weather for food to be grown and harvested to help Britain and the Allies to victory.

Less than two years after the end of the Second World War, 1947 opened with the usual winter weather and on our farm the cattle were all indoors, enjoying more comfort that those of us who carried baskets of turnips and forkfuls of hay to feed them three times a day.

In the fields we were preparing for the spring sowing. To help us out we had engaged Philip Quayle, an agricultural contractor, to cart the farmyard manure from the midden to the fields which had grown oats the previous year. There were no mechanical loaders and all the manure had to be handled by men with *graips* (hand-held forks) – in this case my uncle, Philip, and me.

The field to be manured in this way was in the second of the seven-year rotation of crops dictated by draconian and out-dated lease law. It would be used to grow green crops comprising turnips, vegetables ,and potatoes for stock or human feed; these had to be grown once every seven years as a cleaning crop when all noxious weeds were removed.

Once the load was in the field the manure was dragged off with a *graipling*, a tool with a long wooden handle and four steel prongs set at right angles, and dropped into *pollags*, little mounds of half a dozen forkfuls, to be spread at a later date.

The *pollags* in their parallel lines looked like soldiers on parade (nowadays, modern muck spreaders top dress the field in one operation and there is not a *graip* in sight). The manure would be ploughed in twice, once in winter with a second cross-ploughing in spring. After that the soil would be cultivated to provide a seed bed.

With the coming of tractors any backlog of ploughing could be caught up with in the lengthening days of spring. Previously, with horses for the field work, the manure-spreading and the subsequent ploughing of stubble needed to be completed by Christmas or the work would be well behind schedule. Now, with the

61

power of our Fordson tractor and Philip's International, we had few worries that we would be ready for the spring sowing, even if we did not start carting manure until early January.

In late January there were some snow showers, more than usual, and a frost set in – hard enough to cause the cancellation of most of the ploughing matches. In time they were abandoned for the season, because you cannot get a plough into iron-hard land. Yet no one realised that this was just a taste of things to come. Let my diary tell the story:

February 7th: Severe frost. Spells of drifting snow in east wind. Travel by road possible only in cars and vans fitted with tyre chains.

February 13th: Complete cover of land has stopped all arable work. Stocks of turnips in shed for cattle running low.

February 22nd: Fuel crisis throughout country due to miners strike. We spend our time sawing wood for burning and are giving some to neighbours.

February 25th: Big blizzard from 8pm. Young Farmers were at Knockaloe for stock judging competition in afternoon and tea in Peel. In the evening, in Marown Church Hall for an inter-club debate, the meeting was halted and we were advised to set out for home without delay. Most of us were travelling by motor coach. Neither the Northern or Southern club coaches got very far and were marooned in snow drifts until next day. Those of us with Eastern reached Onchan where Robert Corkill, of Corkill's Garage, who supplied the coach, had two cars fitted with snow chains ready to take home members from further in the country as far as Laxey and Ballaragh.

March 5th: Still no work possible in the fields. Even trimming hedges is difficult because the sides of the three hedges in every field are completely blocked up with frozen snow. To get to the field itself involves trudging through deep snow.

March 11th: It is six weeks today since the beginning of the hard frost, snow and very cold weather. So great is the hold-up in farm work that we have not ploughed a single furrow. The *pollags* of manure have been buried in snow with barely the tops visible. We were fortunate to thresh two stacks of oats before the weather stopped the movement of the travelling threshing outfits, and we are comparatively well off for fodder. Feeding sheep is difficult and we have turned the flock onto one of our two turnip fields where they are managing to scratch through to the top half of the turnips at least.

March 12th: Fresh blizzard from 1pm.

March 16th: Summer time begins. Heavy rain dispels much of the lying snow, but makes no impact on frozen drifts still as high as the hedges.

March 27th: Today we make a belated start on ploughing, but snow drifts still prevent ploughing of headlands.

April 13th: Double summertime begins, so it will be light later in the evenings and we will be staying on the fields longer. However, we have now finished ploughing 30 acres of land and have started harrowing for crops of corn and potatoes.

At last, in mid-April, the severe weather gave way to milder, yet wetter, conditions. When the snow eventually cleared it was revealed that thousands of sheep, especially on the hills, had perished. Losses were estimated to be as high as during the legendary big snow of 1895. The difference was that there was just one huge blizzard in 1895, which caught farmers and flockmasters completely without warning, but this time the snow continued for six weeks with no respite between falls and far more severe frost.

Once in the ground the crops flourished through a miracle of nature, but it took livestock months of summer grazing to regain bodily condition and health. The Island's sheep population was not restored to its previous numbers until two years later.

By June 15th the farm work had eased to the extent

that 35 YFC members were able to embark for Liverpool by steamer for an educational tour of the North of England. There was much relief and joy at this, because only a few weeks earlier there had been talk of cancelling the trip because of the urgency of the spring work. Now we had much to discuss and to learn as we visited the best farms from Lancashire to Durham.

Food shortages continued after the war until 1954, when the last ration books were cast aside, so it was still vital that the land should produce to capacity. Teaching young farmers to farm well was a priority.

Bread had not been rationed during the war in the UK or the Isle of Man, so it was a shock when, on August 28th 1946, Tynwald introduced a scheme where it would be available only on the surrender of coupons, as with other necessities. There was a sudden shortage of wheat for milling into flour, and panic buying of bread. The government was anxious to ensure fair distribution. Fortunately, unlike in the UK, there was no further need to introduce rationing, although supplies were limited and queues often built up outside bakers' shops.

A problem for me was that Billy, our road pony, had a habit of coming to an abrupt halt – no matter how fast he was trotting in the shafts of a float through Onchan – at William Quirk & Sons' shop in Main Road. He knew he was sure of a piece of bread or a bun there, from the shop assistants, sisters Aggie and Renee Roberts. Billy's impatience made him difficult for me to control, and one of the girls always had to leave off serving to provide a tit-bit before he would move. This often brought complaints from customers who were not pleased about Billy taking priority.

I was beginning to attend the farming dinners where men (yes, women were never allowed into this last bastion of male supremacy) made the headlines in the press by making outrageous statements, especially in attacking Tynwald members and civil servants.

The Board of Agriculture was the main target of the few bold enough to stand up in public before a gathering of 200 or more, plus reporters from the four Island newspapers, at such dinners as those organised by the Farmers' Club and the Isle of Man Agricultural Society.

One story which remained fresh, despite the many times I heard it, told of two men standing on the deck of a Steam Packet ship as it pulled into Douglas harbour. One man pointed to something in the sea and asked: 'Look, what's that, Tom?' His companion replied: 'It's a board.'

'Ah well, it can't be the Board of Agriculture - it's moving.'

Most of the after-dinner speakers had gained their experience as Methodist lay preachers on 'the plan', where they were well practised in the pulpit twice each Sunday. As secretary of the Isle of Man Federation of Young Farmers' Clubs, and an occasional contributor to the local press, I was frequently invited to speak – way down the toast list. I did so with great nervousness, not sleeping for nights before such awesome occasions, but persevering and being comforted by the maxim: 'Well, if they've asked me, they must want me.'

The Young Farmers movement was a great training ground for public speaking and gave many of us the confidence we lacked.

The power of the press was evident from the reporting of the farming dinners. Speakers were picked for the vehemence of their opinion on various matters and the newspapers never missed the opportunity to make the most of the occasion. The *Isle of Man Times*, under its editor and proprietor George J. A. Brown, was blatantly anti-agriculture and reflected its attitude in headlines such as '£500,000 more for farmers' – its screaming reply to an announcement of more government subsidies.

Reporting the same speeches, the more moderate *Isle of Man Examiner*, *Mona's Herald* and *Ramsey Courier* would run stories informing their readers that food would be cheaper because of government help towards its production.

End of an era. From April 1st 1955, all Manx-produced cattle, sheep and pigs ready for meat had to go direct to the abattoir, either in Douglas or Ramsey instead of being sold through the three marts. This picture was taken after the last fatstock had been graded in Ramsey Mart on March 30th. Front row: Kathleen Aitken (nee Chrystal) in charge of the office, Stanley Cubbon, butcher and grader, Fred and Turner Chrystal, auctioneers, Joe Leece, farmer and grader and Margaret Davidson (nee Lace), office staff. Others of Chrystal's staff are - Middle: Jimmy Kissack, Don Thompson, Sydney Bryan. Back: Frank Harrison, Jackie Howland, Charlie Gill, Paddy Connor.

With no regular farming features in the Manx press until 1957, when the *Isle of Man Examiner* launched a weekly page edited by Sean Kenny and invited me to contribute, farming news was sporadic. The dinners promoted by 'the Club', now Isle of Man Farmers' Ltd., and the Agricultural Society, were the main source of farming stories. Neither are held nowadays.

Perhaps no one has the patience any longer to sit through a dozen or more speeches, each plugging a particular view. The Farmers' Club dinner was held for years on a Saturday afternoon in December, in Collinson's Cafe, Strand Street, Douglas, beginning at 1pm. Speakers would still be in full flow at 7pm. The men sat back enjoying the cigars on offer, together with Heron & Brearley's bottled beer which even the Methodists, forgetting the pledge they had signed, accepted because it was free. Meanwhile, the women-folk would have come to town with them to do their Christmas shopping.

Farming, both in the fields and in its other activities, was predictable in its timing. So were the Island's other main revenue-earning industries, tourism and fishing. Together they guaranteed the survival of the Manx community.

14
FORTRESS MANN

The Isle of Man can be proud of the fact that while foot-and-mouth has raged elsewhere, this dreaded scourge of livestock has been kept out of the Island, since 1883 at least. During three major outbreaks of foot-and-mouth in the UK, in 1952, 1967-8 and 2001, extreme vigilance has ensured that the Island remained clear and kept its high animal health status.

Rarely fatal, the disease is, however, so contagious or infectious that one case on a Manx farm could spread rapidly to ruin our whole agricultural industry. Although humans, horses, dogs and cats can carry the virus, it has serious consequences only for cloven-hoofed animals, cattle, sheep, pigs and goats. Its rare appearance in humans causes merely a 'flu-type illness.

The Island's splendid isolation (complete with rigid port controls) in recent years has made sure the disease has not spread here, although there must always be worries that our fortress is not impregnable. Unfortunately similar controls for sheep scab, last known in the Isle of Man in 1937, and warble fly, which farmers thought they had eradicated in the 1960s, broke down when both were recognised in recent years in Manx flocks and herds.

The symptoms of foot-and-mouth are that cloven-footed creatures become dull, refuse food, have a drop in milk production, have difficulty in walking and sometimes develop a fever. Lesions are found in the mouth and in the feet and if not slaughtered soon, animals become debilitated and lose condition.

There is no known cure, although the disease is unlikely to cause an animal's death in itself. Its danger lies in its virulence and speed of spread to other cloven-hoofed animals, even miles away, which has led to a theory that it may be airborne.

Foot-and-mouth, or another similar disease, rinderpest, was first noticed in the Isle of Man in 1865. The Lieutenant Governor, Lord Loch, issued a proclamation prohibiting importation of livestock without quarantine. A few months later he banned all fairs and markets for the time being.

In 1865 it was stated that many animals, especially cattle, showed these symptoms; great depression of the vital powers, salivating, staggering gait, cold extremities, quick and short breathing, drooping head and reddened eyes. Animals have discharges from the eyes and also from the nostrils of a mucous nature. There are raw-looking places on the inner side of the lips and roof of the mouth.

But was it foot-and-mouth or rinderpest? Both were new to Manx farmers, nor did the Manx government know much about either. Rinderpest, sometimes known as cattle plague, produces similar symptoms to foot-and-mouth, but the main difference is that nine out of 10 infected cattle usually die. In 1865-66 rinderpest killed 324,000 cattle in the UK, and it could easily have reached the Isle of Man in imported animals.

Lord Loch's first proclamation was issued on September 1st 1865, followed by a second on

September 4th. Both were vague about the specific disease. They prohibited the importation of cattle without quarantine and ordered the slaughter of infected animals but not, as nowadays, of those which had been in contact.

In November that year, local farmers banded together to form the Farmers' Club, still operating 136 years later as Isle of Man Farmers Ltd. at Richmond Hill, Braddan. At the inaugural meeting in the British Hotel in Douglas it was reported that Mr. Allan of Ballavarry, Andreas, had had his complete herd destroyed by disease, not once but twice – it seems that the disease was more likely to have been rinderpest than foot-and-mouth.

'The Club' complained that not enough was being done to overcome farmers' problems with animal health. At a meeting in Castletown on October 10th, Sir James Gell called for more stringent controls because the mystery disease was not abating. The clamour for action led to the government passing its first Cattle Diseases Prevention Act in 1865, and updating it the following year. The acts recognised for the first time that foot-and-mouth as a disease had reached epidemic level not only throughout the Manx countryside but also in the towns and villages where many milking cows were kept.

Rinderpest was dropped from the official documents and in 1877 it was announced that it had been finally eradicated from Europe. It still occurs, however, in Asia and Africa.

Another serious outbreak of animal disease hit the farming industry in the Isle of Man in 1875, and this was foot-and-mouth without a doubt; the government proclamation referred to it by name. First news of the outbreak in 1875 came on October 19th, when the police received reports that 14 cattle belonging to Mr Siddons, of Pulrose Farm – now covered by the housing estate and golf course – had foot-and-mouth disease. Nearby, four sheep owned by Mr Bates of the Quarter Bridge Inn, and sheep kept by Parson Drury, vicar of Braddan, showed signs too.

Hopes of confining the outbreak to Braddan were dashed when the news came that Frank Twigg, a farmer whose name appears as a frequent winner at Manx agricultural shows, had five sheep confirmed as diseased at Bishopscourt Farm, Kirk Michael. The Farmers' Club was requested to send representatives to confer with a committee comprising High Bailiff J. G. Bennett, W. Kneale CP and P. Killey, but the farmers' spokesman failed to turn up at the meeting.

On October 28th, the government ordered port inspection of all incoming animals. From Peel came a report from Captain Munro that he had landed 33 cattle loaded in Ireland. Of these, two were for John Senogles, Clybane, Braddan, and one each for Mr. Cairns, Ballabunt, Braddan and John Clarke, Corvalley, Marown. All four cattle were found to have foot-and-mouth disease.

From the same shipment, others for R. Watson, West Mount, Mount Murray, and Thomas Cretney, Balladhoo, Lonan, were declared healthy and allowed to continue to the farms. Only the infected cows were slaughtered – the highly contagious nature of the disease had not yet been recognised.

At Ramsey, the schooner *Three Brothers* brought in the complete farm stock for Andrew Milligan from Dromore in Scotland. Described in the press of the day as a noted cattle doctor, Milligan had taken Ballasholague, between Ramsey and Laxey. His herd of 18 cattle were put into quarantine in the Old Brewery in Tower Street, Ramsey, but he was allowed to take to Ballasholague three horses, nine sheep, three pigs, one goat, several fowl including pigeons, and a blackbird in a cage. After six days the cattle were confirmed clear of disease and released. But elsewhere in the Island foot-and-mouth was spreading. A Mr. Lorimer, of Mount Rule, Braddan, had imported sheep with the disease and sold some to Mr A. Allison, of Park Llewellyn, Maughold.

The Northern Farmers' Club, which attracted big support during its five years of existence from 1873 to

1878, met in the Mitre Hotel, Ramsey, on October 2nd to discuss the threat to their livestock.

By December 4th they were not satisfied that sufficient measures were being taken to control the spread of foot-and-mouth. They decided to send an urgent letter to the Governor, and meet again on December 18th to consider his reply. Apparently none was forthcoming and the meeting was subsequently cancelled, perhaps because the outbreak was gradually petering out.

For a few years farmers were lulled into a false sense of security, but in 1882 foot-and-mouth was again confirmed on farms near Douglas. Its full impact is not fully recorded. Nevertheless, it continued until February 1883 at least, when Governor Spencer Walpole issued an order prohibiting cattle movements in four areas infected with the disease: Onchan, from Parkfield to Cronkbourne Village; Braddan Bridge to Quarter Bridge to Saddle Road and up to Braddan Vicarage on the road to the Cooil; Nunnery Howe, Kewaigue, St. Mark's, Union Mills, the Strang, Sir George's Bridge through Onchan Village to Onchan harbour; and the mouth of the Laxey river in Lonan to the Dhoon, following the water course known as The Dreem.

It was in that area, from Braddan to Laxey, that the last outbreak of foot-and-mouth occurred on Manx soil. Once conquered, there is no evidence that it ever returned. However, I remember talking as a boy in the 1930s to at least one man who could remember that 1883 outbreak . . .

It was a sunny August day with hardly a breath of wind to wave the standing corn. Three sweating men and a teenager were sitting by a stone-and-sod hedge eating jam sandwiches and drinking tea. They were enjoying afternoon lunch brought to the field at 3pm, a welcome break from 'cutting roads' around a corn field to allow access with the horse-drawn binder.

We were the harvest staff at Ballabeg Farm. My uncle cut the standing corn, swinging the scythe with rhythmic strokes. I was the boy 'making bands' out of the cut corn. Albert Sayle, the horseman, lifted the corn, gathering enough in his arms to form a sheaf and laid it on the band I had placed on the ground. Jack Cowell tied the sheaf with the band and stood it by the hedge.

Jack was in his 70s, a nomadic worker looking for a day or more on a farm in-between other jobs such as doorman and cleaner at some place of entertainment in Douglas during the busy summer season.

'We had foot-and-mouth disease in the Isle of Man in my younger days, you know,' he told us in a subdued voice, as though he was breaking bad news. 'I never want to see it again. It ruined many a farmer, and my father couldn't get work on farms for almost a year.'

Jack was old enough on that day to remember the 1883 foot-and-mouth outbreak, and also to recall one remarkable escape. 'At Sulby Farm in Onchan it was, they had a valuable Shorthorn bull. Came from some duke's herd in England. They never had foot-and-mouth on the farm but it was all around, from Braddan to Laxey. One man did nothing else but look after that bull, and he stayed well away from the cows.

'He kept a change of clothing in a shed alongside the bull's loose-box, and no one else was allowed near that part of the yard. He fed and watered it himself and that bull never got foot-and-mouth.'

I have been unable to find any trace of the story in the press of the day but it stands the test of folklore handed down from one generation to another. It must have been at that time that farmers first realised the terrible virulence of foot-and-mouth as a disease, but sadly I never had a chance to discuss this important feature of animal health with Jack Cowell. He died soon after that memorable day in the corn field.

Restrictions were imposed in the Isle of Man during two other major outbreaks of foot-and-mouth disease in the UK during the 20th century. The 1952 outbreak occurred during the height of the tourist season, the main revenue earner at the time, and any attempts to turn away visitors would have been unthinkable.

The vast numbers of visitors pouring into the

Island from all over the UK posed a huge risk, but the disinfection practices adopted at Ronaldsway Airport and the sea ports kept the disease at bay. The outbreak began in July and five days before the Southern Agricultural Show was due to be held at Castletown on July 31st, the Board of Agriculture banned the exhibition of cattle, sheep and pigs, the cloven-hoofed species susceptible to the disease. Horses, poultry, dogs, cats and rabbits were allowed.

A week later, on August 7th, the one-day Royal Manx Show due to be held at Ramsey suffered a similar fate. The organisers had more time to substitute other attractions in place of the missing animals, and sheaf-pitching and tractor trailer-reversing competitions proved popular.

However the marts at Ramsey, Ballasalla and St. John's went on without interruption on a weekly basis, and the outbreak had waned in time for the autumn sales of sheep and store cattle to take place.

The 1967-68 outbreak resulted in the destruction of 442,000 animals. It began on October 26th in Shropshire and once more strict controls were ordered in the Isle of Man. As the situation worsened, even more stringent conditions were imposed. The two remaining weekly marts, Ramsey and St. John's – Ballasalla had closed for good by then – were shut down for almost three months. All other farming events, including the full ploughing match season which in those days was held in December and January, were abandoned.

It was Monday, January 22nd 1968, before Ramsey mart reopened and St. John's began selling again on the following Wednesday. The first social event of the winter, the Easter YFC dinner, was held in the Palace Hotel, Douglas, on February 27th after its postponement from December 1967. The scare covered Christmas and the New Year and farmers, their families and workers, advised not to leave their farms, had to spend a quiet festive season.

It was March 1968 before country life returned to normal but thankfully it was the last time until 2001 that regulations were needed. An outbreak in the Isle of Wight in 1981 was contained after that island and surrounding parts of Hampshire and Dorset were sealed off.

The beginning of the 21st century, of course, was to bring the worst UK outbreak of all. It led to the slaughter of 3,806,000 sheep, 594,000 cattle, 142,000 pigs and 2,000 goats on 2,030 farms, mainly in Cumbria and Devon. It cost the UK Government about £3 billion. Even more than farming and its ancillary industries, tourism suffered badly too.

The Isle of Man's splendid isolation saved it once more, coupled with strict controls at all the ports of entry. Many major events were cancelled, including, controversially, the TT Races and both summer agricultural shows.

The precautions were strict and brought complaints from the general public that they were inconvenienced in the narrow interests of the agricultural industry. But the defences held, and the Isle of Man has now remained clear of foot-and-mouth since 1883.

15
CAR CONKS AFTER ROYAL VISIT

Loneliness is a feature of farm life. With fewer people than ever working in the industry it is not unusual nowadays to find one man on 200 acres and not another soul in sight. Fifty years ago there would have been half a dozen men on the same land, yet isolation was probably more pronounced. At least today it is easy to find company if you want it in the age of the car.

Often when we arrived home from a Saturday night in town we might not see another outsider ('not a face of clay' was the expression) until the following Saturday. There might be a concert or social in a local hall if we were lucky, and some of the more pious went to church or chapel. We might visit friends or relatives too, but generally the week centred around the farm and its work.

We kept in touch with the outside world through the wireless – all BBC in the days before Radio Luxembourg and, much later, Manx Radio. Television was still a dream, but I for one was an avid reader of the four local newspapers, the national press, and every farming journal I could lay my hands on as well as a weekly library book.

The farm would have visitors, far more than nowadays, but if you were working in the fields you rarely saw them, not even the postman pedalling his way around the parish. A farm was never left unattended. The men might be in the fields, but there would always be one or two women in the house or around the yard.

The practice of leaving someone 'about' even extended to special days, such as the Island's two summer agricultural shows. The men and women would attend one show or the other but someone had to stay home to 'keep an eye on the place' as well as do the milking and attend to other chores.

Today, with the farmer's wife and daughters having jobs off the farm, it is often difficult to find anyone at home and on show days and other occasions the farmer has to do the work when he gets home. Rarely will he have any staff for it.

In the past three or four 'travellers', as we called the representatives from Manx and mainland firms, would come to the farm each week. Those from the local merchants called weekly or fortnightly, always on the same day of the week – you could set your watch by the time of their arrival. Companies off the Island, however, sent reps around once, twice or more a year, selling grass seeds or animal medicines. Farmers tended to segregate them into those they wanted to see because they were essential to the farm's business, and those they wanted to avoid, occasionally because they owed them money.

According to one story a young man on his first visit to the Island relied on names he carried in a pocket notebook used for booking orders (those little books were the hallmark of every traveller). After he had finished pestering a particular farmer for an order he consulted his book and asked for directions to Mr. Kelly of Ballamoar.

'You want to see Mr. Kelly, do you, young man?' enquired the farmer. 'Yes, he's next on my list.' The farmer took out a watch from his waistcoat pocket and looked at it. 'Then you'd better hurry up. They're burying him in half an hour.'

The agents for reliable firms became family friends and their visits were looked forward to for an update on the news from far and wide, but other callers peddled products seldom used, particularly when a customer had to order them in boxes of a dozen.

The animal remedies came in a variety of colours and bottles of strange design. Their names suggested their value, such as Tipper's Vitalis – one of the best, incidentally. Others claimed to cure a variety of ailments including several listed as being suitable for both constipation and diarrhoea, all in the same bottle! Many a farm accumulated dozens of bottles, often bought by the farmer just to get rid of travellers. In recent years, of course, the old bottles have been in demand from people who collect them as a hobby.

The services of the local merchants, and some from the UK or Ireland, were greatly appreciated, although Manx companies complained about their visiting rivals, accusing them of contributing nothing to the Island's economy and not even paying rates on the properties local firms needed. The local firms bought and sold from farmers, while most of the others offered no contra trade. Accounts were settled once a year around Hollantide, when the farmer had sold corn from the harvest and beef, lamb, milk, potatoes and vegetables produced in summer. The money accrued was used to pay for the seeds and fertiliser bought in spring.

It was said that if the biggest agricultural merchants, Corlett Sons & Cowley of Douglas and Ramsey, had closed its books and called in outstanding debts in the depressed 1930s, half the farmers in the Isle of Man would have been made bankrupt. Other firms, including the Farmers Combine in Ramsey, J.R. Riley, T. W. Kelly & Son, Clague & Craine and the Farmers' Club in Douglas, were equally helpful by not pressing for payment. Modern accounting procedures, of course, dictate that credit for such long terms no longer operates.

Other regular visitors to farms were the dealers buying and selling cattle, sheep, horses and pigs. Again they fell into two categories: those who could be trusted and those who could not. Many farmers and dealers traded with each other for years, the dealers acting, like the agricultural merchants, as a bank. There are families who still say that they would not be in farming today had it not been for the animals supplied on credit by such helpful dealers as Dan Creer of Crosby and brothers Frank and Charlie Crowe of Kirk Michael.

But the livestock trading attracted a variety of characters, some even buying animals on farms, taking them off and never returning with their cash or cheques. A few of the local dealers were not above a trick or two, such as one group of four, never seen together in public, who toured the Island seeking stock to buy. Individually they called on a farmer and offered a ridiculously low price for, say, a bunch of young cattle. At first the farmer would reject the offer as totally unacceptable, but by the time the fourth dealer called and suggested even less a man in the depths of the countryside might began to think that this must be their true value. He would sell in case any further offers were lower still.

The syndicate would then share the spoils when they passed the cattle on to another buyer more conversant with current prices.

Walter Jackson, the Manx government's sheep inspector, paid regular visits to every flock, around 1,000 in number, in the 1940s. His job was to watch out for sheep scab, a disease which causes distress to the animals and loss of income to farmers and flockmasters. He had led the campaign to eradicate it, culminating in the Battle of Greeba in 1937 when a posse of police marksmen shot a group of feral sheep hiding in the plantation and proving uncatchable. The Island stayed clear until 1997, when sheep scab reappeared through some laxity in vigilance and import restriction. Mr. Jackson, who never drove a car, used to travel by bus – on which he had a pass – and on foot to visit every flock in the Island.

He lived at the remote Park Llewellyn in the shadow of North Barrule. One of his routes involved getting off the Ramsey-to-Douglas bus at our gate on the White Bridge Hill approaching Onchan, from where he walked overland, calling at flocks on the way, and reaching Crosby to catch a bus on his return home via Douglas. Sunday was no day of rest for he travelled far to country chapels as a Methodist preacher. Mr. Jackson's grandson, Ellwood Parsons, carries on the family tradition as a farmer on a huge area of lowland and hill and is the immediate past president of the Manx National Farmers' Union.

When the union was formed in 1946 it was considered a belated effort by farmers to be heard in the political arena. England and Wales as one national union, and Scotland and Ulster each with its own union, had been operating for many years. There was no official voice of the farmer except the Farmers' Club (Isle of Man Farmers today) but it was not fully representative of the industry.

In 1947, a year after its launch, the union's membership stood at 506, less than half the number of practising farmers, and a recruiting drive was instituted. Deemster Ramsey Johnson was the virtual founder but handed over the role of president to Clifford Kniveton, farmer turned businessman as the owner of a quarry at Ballasalla supplying lime to farmers and stone to the construction industry.

In October 1947, when an abundant potato crop was being lifted despite late planting after a severe winter, the union council considered a proposal that farmers should withhold all potatoes from the market until the Governor's Executive Council raised the controlled price of 9/- per hundredweight.

It was the first test of the solidarity of farmers, but came to nothing because about half their number kept on selling potatoes, taking over the customers normally supplied by the strikers.

There was internal disagreement within the union over the price of oats, then the main cereal crop with 14,000 acres sown.

Although most of the Island's 1,200 separate farms were run on a mixed system, with each growing something of everything and keeping all four species of farm livestock as well as large flocks of free range hens, the grain-growing land was in the south or on the northern plain. The main concentrations of cattle, especially those kept for milk production and sale, were in the centre.

The union's council consisted of delegates from each of the 17 parishes, plus half a dozen co-opted members. Livestock farmers wanted to buy oats for cattle, sheep, pigs and – still – horses, as cheaply as possible. The farmers with extensive arable acres devoted to oats were looking for a high return when they sold to the merchants, whose customers were the livestock men. So the union tried to balance the widely divergent views of its members, not always successfully.

Outsiders said that the only time farmers agreed was once a week in chapel and then only because their wives were alongside them! But despite differences at the political level, there was still a wonderful degree of neighbourliness in the heart of the countryside. No one ever let any bad feeling stop one farmer helping another at busy seasons or in emergencies, and 'help' on mill days when a crew of 15 was required for threshing was never refused.

Unfortunately much of the dissension among farmers reached the public arena through Tynwald or the press, and all sections used it to their benefit. Yet few people heard about the case of one farmer who had the reputation of being a cussed fellow who quarrelled with practically everyone.

When he died suddenly one mid-winter in the 1930s, his widow, who wanted to stay at the farm until the following November, was faced with the prospect of ploughing and sowing all the crops. She had only enough men to look after the livestock. The neighbours rallied round, and each sent a man with a pair of horses to help her.

The King and Queen, George VI and Queen Elizabeth – now the Queen Mother – came to Onchan on July 4th 1945. Three of us went from Ballakilmartin in our ancient Morris Oxford to see them outside the Avenue Cinema in Royal Avenue, Onchan, the most elegant building in the village. After all royalty could hardly be welcomed outside the commissioners' office, then on the Douglas side of the Manx Arms, for alongside the entrance stood the ladies and gents toilets – just as they still do today.

Taking the car meant using some of our precious petrol ration which had been increased to five gallons a month on June 1st – we could now indulge in 'pleasure motoring', we were told. We thought we had enough in the tank, but returning home up the Whitebridge Hill the old car conked out for want of it. I had to walk home to the farm to pick up an empty petrol can, walk back to Corkill's Garage where Robert Corkill allowed me one gallon from the next month's ration, and back again to the stranded car. We might as well have walked in the first place.

16
ENVYING ENGLISH PRICES

'English prices and conditions' was the slogan adopted by some of the leaders of the Manx farming community in 1948. But just as many opposed the idea, typical of a deeply divided industry. UK farmers were on a roll, in modern parlance, following the adoption of a new Agriculture Act at Westminster. It guaranteed them a fair return on everything they grew, and gave them first call on the food market. The 1947 Act was considered by many observers as the finest piece of countryside legislation ever enacted. Many still hold that view.

Tom Williams, Minister of Agriculture in the Labour Government which unexpectedly defeated Churchill's Tories at the general election shortly after the war, was the architect of the new Act. He declared, 'The land is our biggest asset, and we must make full use of it. We cannot afford to do otherwise.'

The subsidies paid to farmers to support their industry, at first a wartime measure to encourage food production, were retained in the new legislation. Not everyone supported the subsidy system and one outspoken Labour politician, Stanley Evans, lost his post as a junior minister by describing farmers as 'featherbedded', a label that has stuck to this day.

The Isle of Man in general envied the prosperity of UK farmers, and the Government invited Tom Williams to the Island for talks. The public had a chance to meet him when he attended the Isle of Man Agricultural Show at the Nunnery on August 7th.

On the Corlett Sons & Cowley machinery stand Mr. Williams climbed onto the 'board' of a new threshing mill and fed the first sheaf board of corn through it. We farm-fed lads were more intrigued by the winged white collar and trilby hat he wore than by his ability to fill a place in a mill crew.

Food was still desperately short and only the practices of adding potato flour to bread and eating horse meat kept the nation from starving, although we were not told this at the time. Manx prices lagged behind those UK farmers received, and the aim in some quarters was to enact legislation similar to the 1947 UK Agriculture Act. That was where the clamour for 'English prices and conditions' came in.

However, the two food markets were dissimilar and opponents declared that the same price ranges could not operate – adding that they were also against selling out to the English. The main differences, of course, lay in demand. In the UK food was required for virtually the same number of consumers each week in the year. In the Isle of Man the population doubled during the summer tourist season, from June to September. Farmers timed their greatest production of milk for those three months, and to encourage them farm prices of milk were higher on the Island in summer and lower in winter,

The English scale was the reverse. There, price differentials encouraged production of different foods needed for summer. There were many arguments about which was the better system for the Isle of Man.

Unlike nowadays, the Labour party had a lot of support from farmers, although most parted company with it on the question of the nationalisation of the land. Government ownership smacked to Manx farmers of a return to the Derby and Stanley eras, and was too much akin to Russian communism. Yet in Young Farmers' debates on the subject, nationalisation often won the vote, such was the dissatisfaction and frustration among young people unable to obtain a farm of their own.

Milk was a commodity in particularly erratic supply. Sometimes in the summer season there was not enough for the huge demand of an extra 60,000 visitors, and the Isle of Man Dairies would have to import supplies in 10-gallon churns as deck cargo on the Steam Packet ships. Then at either end of the summer there would be a surplus; cows peaked in output on the rich May grass, and again in September when the holidaymakers had returned home.

For a few years there was a milk shortage in England as farmers struggled to rebuild their herds following wartime reductions in cattle numbers. It had often been more expedient then to kill cows for meat rather than milk them. In times of shortage in England the trade would be reversed, and Manx milk was exported to Liverpool. Around 80 farmers delivered milk daily to the Isle of Man Dairies depot in Spring Gardens, Douglas. If we were there around 8am after milking our cows by hand, we lads were sometimes pressed into service to help load the heavy kegs onto the motor lorries. We even carried some in our own vehicles in the mad rush to catch the 9am boat for Liverpool. As in swapping help with other farmers, we never counted the hours or expected pay for the extra work. Some of the exported milk was carried by air, but we never had the excitement of a trip to Ronaldsway. Since 1985 all milk has been collected from Manx farms by road tankers, except for those producers retailing their own.

Our landlord at Ballakilmartin wanted to found a dairy herd at another of his farms, Ballafreer at Union Mills, and decided to bring in a shipment of cows from the Republic of Ireland. They were Shorthorns, red, roan and white in colour, and he decided to sell 27 he did not need at auction on May 6th 1948.

The cows were tuberculin-tested which entitled them to be described as TT. They were offered for sale at an unusual venue – behind the TT Grandstand, so we had TT cows sold at the home of TT races.

I would not have dared say so his face because the relationship between landlord and tenant was always delicate, but the cows were real butchers' beasts, very fat and bereft of any milking qualities. We were not surprised. After all, Mr. Quirk was a butcher and he selected the cows himself. Nevertheless at auction to Manx farmers they reached a top price of £84, and the 27 made an average of £53.

In the years after the war there was a chance that sheep dog trials might earn as much fame for the Isle of Man as its motorcycle races. The idea came from Deemster Sir Percy Cowley, chairman of the Manx National Sheep Dog Committee, which had George Howie, the Manx Government agricultural organiser, as secretary.

The Tourist Board agreed to pay star handlers with their border collies to come to the Island – starting money you might call it. Howstrake golf course, the scene of a trial which before the war had attracted 8,000 spectators, was to be used again. It was described as among the best locations in Britain because the spectators could see the dogs and sheep at every point of the course, from the gather at the top of the hill to the final penning in front of the grandstand.

The best dogs from England, Scotland, Wales and Ireland gave the trials an international flavour and the holidaymakers could identify themselves with those from their own country. It was even rumoured that there was on-course betting, to which the learned Deemster turned a blind eye despite its illegality under Manx law.

Stewards to look after the sheep were recruited

from the farming community for a trial at Howstrake on July 20th 1947. I was one unpaid volunteer, and it gave me a break from work on the farm as well as a free lunch in the Howstrake Hotel.

During the afternoon of the first day one sheep broke away from a group of six, and before any of the shepherds could be called to retrieve it with a dog it cleared a stone wall and headed in the direction of Douglas. Four of us set off in an old Morris van in pursuit and caught it, believe it or not, near the war memorial on Douglas promenade. The incident did not escape a national newspaper reporter covering the trials. He wrote a story which earned the headline 'Terrified Sheep Chased by Mob', with us four stewards as the 'mob'. In fact when we found the sheep it was puffing a little, but standing quietly amongst a group of holidaymakers who were trying to feed it ice cream.

Trials continued at Howstrake until the operators of the golf course complained that they were losing revenue when it was closed for golf; they increased the rent to a figure the organisers refused to pay.

Later, television would kill sheep dog trials as a crowd-puller. 'One Man and his Dog' was heavily edited and showed only the best performances. Spectators were no longer prepared to stand or sit watching 10 or more dogs in order to see perhaps just one performance of the standard offered on television.

On June 30th 1948, the Isle of Man was invaded by 4,500 Ulster Young Farmers piling off two Steam Packet ships at Douglas harbour. They were on a day trip organised by the Ulster Federation of Young Farmers' Clubs, with disembarkation at noon. The Boards of Agriculture and Tourism on the Island joined to arrange two meals before the evening departure for Belfast.

Manx Young Farmers were called in as guides, and we met them on Victoria Pier with placards carrying different numbers (the trippers had been instructed to join pre-allocated groups). My wife-to-be, Laura Kermode, and I were in charge of a party heading for the Café Royale on King Edward Road. Special horse trams and electric trains were laid on with the change at Derby Castle (now Summerland), and the operation went perfectly smoothly.

But after lunch the party dispersed, many of them to Onchan Head and its showground attractions. They were asked to return to the same cafe for tea at 5.30pm, but unfortunately some became lost and others, once they found the centre of Douglas, did not choose to return to the attractions of the Café Royal. The same happened with other parties destined for other eating places. The result was that a lot of food went uneaten that day, but the establishments lost nothing because the visitors had prepaid for their travel and meals.

The visitors sailed around the Calf of Man on their way here from Belfast, and returned home via the Point of Ayre. It was part of the Steam Packet's contribution to a wonderful day in fine sunny weather. Apparently there is just one mile difference in the two routes but the times for the journeys can be affected by tides.

The meeting with so many Young Farmers from another country was the first of many exchanges between Manx and Ulster members, although never again did they come in such numbers. The chance to talk with others living off the fruits of the land was of benefit to both sides, as we discovered problems which are the same wherever land is farmed.

To this day, friendships between Young Farmers from all over the world have strengthened the base of Manx agriculture and many others who depend on it for a living.

17
CICERO GOT ME FARMING

It took a Roman philosopher to push me into farming. Without his words I might well have begun a hunt for a completely different job when I left school in 1936. At the time there were few opportunities for school leavers, and unless your family had money or you had exceptional brains, your chances of going to college or university were pretty slim.

There was more than enough work in the summer in the tourist trade, but little to look forward to in a long, bleak winter other than the dole and government work schemes, neither of which gave anyone hope of a job for life. My uncle and aunt could offer me work on the farm we lived on at the time, Ballabeg at Cronkbourne. But it was the old story in farming – plenty to do, but little money to pay for it. So I drifted into it rather than making any conscious decision to become a farmer; although it was what I wanted, its future offered little promise.

Those who went into farming were dubbed 'farmer's boy', and often goaded by irreverent wording of the song of the name. We were branded 'farm labourers', but once I found out what a highly skilled job it was I vowed never to use the word labourer in relation to men on farms again. This job demands the ability to work with nature in cultivating the land and tending the needs of livestock, in addition to numerous skills which others spend years learning.

Had not Cicero (106-43BC) written these words? 'Of all things from which gain is received, nothing is better than agriculture, nothing more productive, more delightful, more worthy of a man.'

I had little classical inclination, but this seemed to sum up the type of life I wanted. Long after I had established a toehold on the farming ladder I used to include this quotation in publications concerning the Isle of Man Federation of Young Farmers' Clubs, and it keeps cropping up in public-speaking competitions and wherever young farmers speak or act in public.

But heeding ancient philosophy did not ensure anyone a living from farming, even if many of us, despite years of struggle, consider it the greatest vocation in the world and are loath to quit it for retirement. Farmers paid members of their own families little or nothing, although no one ever went short of food, clothes or shelter. The problem was (and still is) that the young had little chance of saving to rent or buy a farm of their own. There was always the hope of stepping into the boss's wellies, hopefully before he died, but if you succeeded him on retirement you might well have to provide for him and his wife into old age.

In some cases farms have had to be sold to generate money to keep older family members in residential or nursing homes, one of the failures of the welfare state. If you have no money or property the government will do it for you.

The worker with no family in farming may have had ambitions to become a farmer, but more likely he went to work on a farm because it provided him with a job and a home. He would be hired by a farmer at Hollantide and at least was sure of a bed, food and a few bob for the coming year. If married he would be supplied with a tied cottage, to be vacated on the day he left the farm for another job – or worse, for no job at all, when he would have to throw himself on the mercy of the parish.

Only those who worked with such men know how apprehensive, even frightened, they were in the approach to Hollantide. The farmers themselves, 80 % of whom were tenants 50 years ago, often had similar fears towards the end of their leases until eventually in 1968 Tynwald gave them a degree of security in land tenure.

Farm workers were notoriously poorly paid and even the Labour Party, both in the UK and on the Island, was loath to push for higher wages because it would mean that food would be dearer for a party pledged to keep down the cost of living. In the Isle of Man at the end of World War One farm workers began agitation for better wages and conditions. They were led by Charlie Gill of Ballaugh, and they looked to the Workers Union established in Douglas for support.

As an orator capable of rousing any audience, Gill likened affairs in the countryside to the biblical story of seven years of plenty and seven of famine. He said: 'Manx farmers knew the bumper years of 1914 to 1918. They stored their profits in the granary at the end of Athol Street – or the Isle of Man Bank as some call it. Now the lean years have come for the rest of us, but they refuse to distribute the surplus to those who helped them to create their wealth.'

Farm workers now had spokesmen within the Workers Union and in 1920 talks were held with the Isle of Man Farmers' Club, in essence a co-operative trading organisation. Farmers would not have their own political union until 1946.

The talks resulted in the first attempt to fix a recognised minimum wage for the Island's 2,000 employed farm men. Agreement was reached on a rate of 35/- for a 58-hour week without any overtime payment or extra for Sunday or emergency work. When workers still complained, the winter hours were reduced to 51 hours per week.

Eventually Tynwald, after a few hesitant starts, created an Agricultural Wages Board consisting of representatives of employers and employees with an independent chairman. It operates to this day. By 1945 it had fixed the weekly wage at £3.10s. per week, still below the general wage but high enough to avoid exploitation of workers. In that year, according to official figures from the Board of Agriculture, the number of farm workers – including the farmers' sons but not the farmer himself, or his wife – stood at 1,390.

Farming was gradually being mechanised, and we watched men leaving the land as agriculture became more efficient. In 2001 one man can milk 150 cows twice a day in a modern milking parlour. When I started in farming a man (or woman) who could milk eight cows by hand in an hour was eagerly sought.

At the last count, outside of the farmer and his wife who on many farms today are the sole staff, the number of employed men has dropped to 313, hardly as many as in some of the Island's larger firms. There are also an estimated 2,000 people acquiring all or part of their living from farming without actually working on farms.

Farming is unique in encouraging skills on a competitive basis. Ploughing matches have been held in the Isle of Man since 1840 and sheep-shearing competitions began in the early 1930s. Farmers compete against each other to exhibit the best animals and there are annual contests to decide the best crops of silage, hay and grain, as well as to select the leading farms for excellence in both crops and livestock. Competitors learn to assess the merits of livestock at judging competitions, the first of which was held at the Isle of Man Agricultural Show at the Nunnery Park, Douglas, in 1923. Building hedges, erecting fences and handling tractors safely are all skills tested in a well-established programme, particularly in the Young Farmers' Clubs.

I recorded, although I was not aware of it at the time, the gradual mechanisation of the 120 acres we farmed. Here are extracts from my diary:

1943, April 20th: Billy shod at Abbeylands Smithy with full set of shoes. At the same time, I took in a cart, a horse ridging plough for repairs, and brought home a set of harrows after the points had been lain and sharpened.

May 4th: After being on order nine months, our tractor is delivered by E.B.Christian & Company. It is our first tractor, a Fordson on steel wheels and costs £190, a rise of £20 on the original quote.

August 20th: Changing spade lugs on tractor wheels for smaller harvest spuds. The cleats are needed for traction on ploughed fields but will tear up the land when cutting corn.

August 26th: For the first time we use our new tractor to pull the binder cutting a field of oats, replacing three horses. The Albion binder has been fitted with a tractor hitch instead of a horse pole.

November 3rd: We take delivery of a Massey Harris two furrow trailer plough after a long wait and for use behind the tractor. It is supplied by Corlett, Sons & Cowley Limited at a cost of £49 compared with the £14, 12 shillings and nine pence, in April 1942, for our last new horse plough, a Sellar Medium, when we had no intention of buying a tractor.

1944, January 7th: Although our Fordson tractor pulling a two furrow plough has done most of the ploughing we still plough with horses on occasions, mainly to give horses and men some exercise. I hate to admit it but I fear we have too much horse power, real and mechanical, on the farm since we acquired a tractor. Sooner or later we will be forced to part with our beloved horses.

January 18th: Delivering by horse and float turnips to Heron & Brearley in Douglas. The brewery firm still retains four draught horses for transport purposes and it is for them the turnips are required, not to give

additional flavour to the already weak wartime beer.

April 20th: We have borrowed a spreader to sow lime. We obtained six tons of slaked lime in bags and 15 tons of loose lime from Billown Lime Quarries which they delivered. The spreader is pulled by a horse, much more convenient than using the tractor, especially as there are long waits while we fill the spreader by shovel.

April 22nd: We fix two sets of harrows in tandem behind the tractor for working the field for a crop of corn. Using one set the tractor is under-employed.

April 28th: Working until 9pm with two horses in our iron roller I finish the 12 acre Big Garey in one day. Yesterday with the tractor I harrowed the same field twice in four hours but the horses make a neater job for rolling.

April 29th: Carting dung to potato ridges with two carts. We have no trailer for the tractor but will have to look around for one. Several local joiners are making trailers but the farmer has to find the axle and wheels, usually obtainable from a dismantled motor lorry.

May 25th: Blossom, a four-year-old Clydesdale filly, is handled for the first time today prior to being broken to work. We have decided that even with the advent of tractors, horses will always be needed in Manx farming.

November 9th: There is a distinct fall in prices at farm auctions this Hollantide. Horses in particular are in poor demand as more farmers buy tractors.

1945, May 21st: Blossom, our five-year-old pedigree Clydesdale mare, is mated to the Board of Agriculture Clydesdale stallion Balgreen Inheritance. The aim is to breed a foal of showing standard.

October 6th: Harvest completed after the most difficult season, the older folk say, since 1917. Apart from using it to haul the binder, the tractor played no part. Horses and carts, mostly two but sometimes three when a neighbour came to help, moved the corn, all oats, from the field to the stacks we made in the haggart.

1946, April 30th: Blossom, now six years old, foals a colt. When found the foal is already on foot.

1949, May 24: Despite the rush of spring work we have decided to devote time to handling Blossom. We require her to make up a pair of working horses with Prince, a 10-year-old Chestnut gelding. Blossom, like so many horses in this mechanical age, has been neglected, eating her head off at grass. But she is of excellent conformation with good feet and legs and is keen to work. Billy at 30 years old cannot be expected to work much longer. I believe that many jobs can still be done more economically (and certainly more enjoyably) with horses than a tractor and I hope I shall never live to see the horses banished completely from our agriculture. The number of good horses reaching the horse-flesh market is high and surely to be deplored, not only on sentimental grounds but in relation to the economy of the country. How many jobs can still be done more cheaply by a horse than a 50hp tractor using imported fuel?

But it was not to be. Blossom's son never paraded in a show ring. Instead he was bought by a dealer for the English meat market, although Blossom herself lived out her life doing very little work until she died peacefully at pasture through old age.

The coming of combine harvesters to the Isle of Man in 1944 heralded a revolution in which there would no longer be a place for a horse in the corn field.

18

IN PRAISE OF THE COW

They strolled down the lane together,
The sky was studded with stars
They reached the gate in silence
And he lifted down the bars.
She neither smiled nor thanked him
Because she knew not how
For he was just a farmer's boy
And she was a Jersey cow.

Has any animal made more of a contribution to the human race than the humble cow? Those of us who tended them were often ridiculed as being 'tied to a cow's tail', and we were, because she needed feeding three times a day in winter and milking twice daily, summer and winter. But between us we fed the Manx nation before easy transport meant that a peasant in some other country could supply the food. In the 1930s the Manx would have starved without the Shorthorn cow and those who looked after her.

Shorthorns in their magnificent strawberry roan, red or pure white predominated, but there were a few Ayrshire, Friesian, Jersey and Guernsey dairy cows and Aberdeen Angus and Hereford beef animals as well. We had not even heard of the hard-to-spell European breeds.

The milking cows, 8,000 in all throughout the Island, had to be milked by hand twice a day. No wonder we saw little of the outside world and because of our knowledge of life beyond the farm gate were labelled *govags* by those who knew more about, but produced less towards, the economy of our little country.

As early as the 1930s some Manx farmers were experimenting with milking machines, but few had any success. 'Ruination of good cows,' said the majority of people, in and out of farming. 'You can't go against nature.' The trouble was that cows did not take to machine milking after knowing nothing but 'strigging' by hand. They withheld their milk and soon 'went wrong in the bag.' But was taking milk from cows by any manner not against nature? Cows gave milk just for their calves not to share with human beings.

We sat on three-legged stools and sang to our cows as we milked them, and were astonished in the Year of Our Lord 2001 to hear a highly-paid and learned scientist suddenly announce that cows gave more milk when music was played to them. We could have told him that without all the time and expense that went into proving the fact and then going on television to tell us!

One cowman I know reckoned he got more by his rendition of Paul Robeson's 'Ol' Man River'. Another preferred George Formby's 'Riding in the TT Races' as providing the best rhythm for squeezing and pulling a cow's teat. 'Down at the Old Bull and Bush' was also

Black and white dairy cows, formerly called British Freisian, now to be known as Holstein following the amalgamation of the Holstein and Freisian breed societies, have taken over almost completely from Shorthorns in my lifetime. This is a prize-winning heifer from pioneer Freisian breeder, Ian Anderson, haltered by Bryan Kennaugh, his herdsman.

1pm, to enable the delivery man to begin his afternoon round. By mid-September the weather would have resorted to its autumn pattern and we reverted to milking at 5pm.

In 1931 Tynwald passed a new Milk and Dairies Act, which decreed that cowsheds and dairies must be brought up to a standard approved by a Local Government Board inspector. It came as a blow to farm folk, who had always believed that to add to the comfort of a cow every nook and cranny in the cowshed should be stuffed with straw to prevent draughts. The new regulations, however, laid stress on ventilation. Hopper windows that would open air ducts according to the number of cows kept in the stalls had to be fitted. Bovine tuberculosis was rife throughout the Island, and we were told that the humid atmosphere we encouraged helped its spread. A

a cowshed favourite, especially during the summer when the milkers renewed acquaintance with Florrie Forde at the Derby Castle each holiday season.

Every able-bodied man, woman and bigger boy on the farm was expected to milk in the morning before settling down to other work, such was the rush to have the milk warm and frothy, ready for the customer. In summer heat, from May to September, there was a second daily delivery during the afternoon. There was no effective way to keep milk from going sour apart from standing cans in the horse trough with its running water, known to this day as the cooler. So the second milking began on dairy farms at

pity, because the cowshed – cosily warm in winter and a shady retreat in summer – was a place where men could relax. After midday dinner many had a short nap in a bed of straw in an empty stall.

We were constantly having buildings altered to keep up with government regulations. On one occasion our landlord employed three 'foreigners', men working for themselves in the evenings and weekends as masons and joiners. One man had a bulbous red nose, and my aunt remarked, 'I'll bet he's a boozer. A sure sign, a nose like that.' But on Christmas Eve only he turned up for work, on a day they finished early for the holiday at their regular jobs.

A fine example! John Faragher, farm manager at Ballakillingan, Lezayre holding the champion cow from the 1998 Black and White Spring Show. Pictured also are the owner Julian Edwards with the visiting judge.

value of each animal from the Manx Government there would be no compensation for loss of earnings until the farm was re-stocked many months later.

At our first test on April 12th 1951, 16 out of the 39 cattle of all ages failed to pass the test and were condemned for slaughter. On May 3rd I wrote in my journal: 'Twelve of our 16 cattle which reacted to the TB test are collected for slaughter by Leece, the hauliers. It is distressing to see some of our old faithfuls taking their last journey, but we have to move with the times and the Attested Herds Scheme is here to stay in the interests of human health.'

There was a political crisis within the dairy industry in that year, and here is how I reported it at the time in my journal:

July 2nd: Much concern is being expressed by Manx farmers at the action of the Lieutenant Governor Sir Geoffrey Bromet in fixing the price of milk for the next ten months under a Defence of the Realm regulation at a level not acceptable to producers' organisations. The recommendations of these organisations have been completely ignored and the machinery constituted under the Tynwald Marketing Acts for the fixing of farm prices has been bypassed. The price schedule adopted is said to emanate from a civil servant in Government Office and fixes the price of milk at one penny a gallon less than the producers are willing to accept.

The way in which the matter has been handled by

'Where's your pals?' she asked.

'Oh, they got off the bus at the Manx Arms and went in for a drink. They'll be here later.'

'Didn't you go with them?' she probed further.

The man with the red nose drew himself up to his full height and roared, 'Madam, I am a life long teetotaller and intend staying that way!'

It was a crisis year for Manx dairy farmers in 1951. The scheme to eradicate tuberculosis from cattle was in full swing, and like the later foot-and-mouth epidemics in the UK it brought heartbreak for farming families. There was compulsory slaughter of animals, often whole herds, and while farmers received the market

Government Office precipitates a constitutional crisis which will be discussed in Tynwald next week, when questions concerning it will be tabled. Whatever the case for or against an adjustment to milk prices the fact remains that democratic government has no place for this kind of dictatorship directed towards farmers by the so called 'agricultural division' of Government Office.

Roughly, the wholesale price of milk is fixed at 2/10d for summer production and 3/1d for winter, an increase over the year of threepence per gallon. The retail price rises by one penny per quart to 11d all the year round. The summer price is accepted by farmers as sufficient to cover the cost of production when milk can be produced from grass alone but it is necessary to compensate them for the losses during winter. The cost of winter feeding is such that some farmers say they need 5/- per gallon in order to make a living.

Another fine example of a prize cow - Anderson Farms', Ballamoar, Patrick, winning beast at the Royal Manx Agricultural Show in 1994. Left to right: David Anderson (now MHK), Ian Anderson and Bryan Kennaugh, herdsman.

Isle of Man Dairies Ltd., the principal distributing company, are opposed to the new prices which give them a margin of only 8d per gallon, 4d less then they require. While farmers realise that Government Office is endeavouring to make milk production less attractive and beef rearing more remunerative it is generally felt that the present prices will result in a serious shortage of milk and are a let-down for an important section of the agricultural industry.

August 23rd: The dispute over milk prices has now resolved into a state of hostility between Manx farmers and Government Office. The price-fixing machinery set up under the Agricultural Marketing Acts has broken down, and there are no controlled prices for potatoes, wool and cereals. The Manx National Farmers' Union has acted with commendable promptness and has had several meetings to consider the action to be taken to deal with a serious situation. At one of these meetings a resolution was passed to ask the Manx Government to refer the whole question of farm prices to arbitration. The Deputy Governor Deemster Percy Cowley in the absence of Governor Bromet replied that no machinery exists under the Marketing Acts for such a procedure. Considering that Government Office completely ignored the acts in fixing milk prices under the Defence of the Realm Act, this reply only emphasises the dictatorial attitude adopted by our administrators throughout the negotiations.

Farmers generally have been very moderate in their demands and in their action although there are a few rebels who would have sabotaged the Island's other important industry, the tourist trade, by withholding food supplies during the peak weeks of the summer season.

September 17th: The war between Manx farmers and the government has developed into guerilla tactics, with much sniping between the Farmers' Union and government spokesmen in the local press. No satisfactory settlement will be achieved this way, nor is the strike threat by farmers likely to contribute towards a just result. In fact talk of a strike tends to bring the weight of public opinion against the farmers' case.

November 26th: At the Farmers' Club dinner last Saturday the Lieutenant Governor Sir Geoffrey Bromet smooths over many of the differences between Government Office and the farming community in a diplomatic and statesmanlike speech.

He announces that a plan has been formulated in joint discussions to set dairy farming on a more stable footing. The plan guarantees the producer an average annual price of 2/10d per gallon for milk sold wholesale for the liquid market and for the first 20,000 gallons manufactured into cheese or exported each year.

Discussions are still proceeding over the details of the scheme especially about fears voiced by producer retailers who consider that their milk surplus to the requirements of their rounds should be included in the quantity subsidised for manufacture.

One huge change is that the scheme forbids producers to sell milk by wholesale except under a recognised contract with the Milk Marketing Association. A producer will not be permitted to deliver more than the amount specified in his contract and will be allowed, in theory at least, a deviation of 10 % less than the stipulated quantity.

Responsible farming opinion is that the scheme should be given a fair trial although doubts are expressed about its successful operation. Anything, however, is preferable to the disorganised chaos the milk industry has developed into during the past few months.

19
CASHING IN ON TURNIPS

Neighbours moving from farm to farm to lift and carry to the fields cows and younger cattle too weak to get up after a winter of near starvation . . . These were the spectral scenes which used to haunt the Manx countryside during May each year. They were called 'lifting days', and when I was young there were still people around who remembered them. Judging by our ages, the grim ritual was common until around 1880.

By May the grass was growing, and the animals would be able to graze and eventually build up their strength. Any surplus grass during summer was made into hay and built into stacks which were thatched with rushes to keep it dry for feeding to cattle and horses during the long winter.

Before fertilisers were available to boost grass growth, winter feed was scarce. A new departure which increased the supply of livestock food was the introduction of the turnip or swede to the Island. Cattle relish them even if their feeding value is low; they fill their stomachs and satisfy their hunger.

Writing in 1797, Basil Quayle noted that 'turnips have been grown these last few years producing very good crops but great attention has to be paid to their tillage, manuring and hoeing. The potato crop is such a favourite that dung cannot be spared for turnips so few are grown.'

Thomas Quayle, Basil's successor as reporter in the Isle of Man for the UK Board of Agriculture, wrote in 1812: 'About 30 years have elapsed since the introduction of turnips as an article of field culture in the Isle of Man. At present they are extending but not in the degree they merit.' He observed that they were still not in regular use for cattle feed but were valuable for the large number of horses especially any in full work.

Throughout the mid and late 1800s turnips became more popular as farming methods improved; they were soon the staple diet of cattle, together with hay, straw, and imported concentrated feed usually called cake. Oats were grown as the chief grain for cattle and horses in its whole or crushed form, and for humans who cooked it into porridge.

The turnip acreage rose to 8,000 by the end of the 1800s, but there was not enough, even with hay supplies, to adequately nourish all the cattle. By the coming of spring many were so weak that they had to be carried to fields of grass – hence the lifting days.

Turnips are labour-intensive and at the height of their popularity, which continued until the 1950s, this crop occupied farm staffs for almost half of their working hours. The ground for them was manured and ploughed during winter, and cultivated again with a second ploughing in May, when the field would be set up in ridges into which the tiny turnip seed was sown. Six weeks later, a profusion of plants had to be thinned out to leave around one in ten to grow into a turnip during the summer.

For a century-and-a-half there was no way of sowing seed singly to obviate the task of singling. Weeding either by horse hoe or by hand was often necessary in July and August.

From October to April the fully-grown turnips would be pulled, their leaves and roots docked off and carted to the farmstead for feeding to cattle or scattered on the fields for sheep. A supply for around one week would be stored at intervals. They would be fed to cattle three times daily throughout a six-month winter period.

Turnip thinning was a useful source of extra cash for many, but a back-breaking job for most. Here the process is being carried out at an Open Day at Cregneash.

The turnips were carried to the cattle in chip baskets, some being offered whole to cows with good teeth. Older cows who had lost their teeth, and younger animals whose teeth had not yet grown, needed to have the turnips chopped, in my early days by crushing them with a masher but for most of the time that I remember by a turnip cutter turned with a handle.

The Isle of Man has a perfect climate for turnip production. As well as food for livestock, Manx-grown turnips were eagerly sought in markets in the north of England. By the time they reached the housewife they were described as 'swedes grown in the healthy soils of the Isle of Man set in the middle of the Irish Sea', a good selling point amidst the smoke and grime of the industrial towns. It was a cash crop the farmer welcomed, although none of us involved looked forward to the rush of activity during bitter winter weather to dock the turnips, put them into bags which had to be stitched securely, and move them to an access point for the buyers' lorries.

Demand was always highest in spells of frost and snow when few other vegetables were available in England.

Turnips did not offer themselves to the early days of mechanisation of agriculture. The tractor took some of the heavy work out of cultivation, but was too cumbersome to operate between the turnip ridges until Harry Ferguson developed his smaller and lighter Ferguson TE 20 on rubber tyres. The nightmare of a tractor driver was the risk of removing in one fell swoop a growing row of turnips which had taken almost a year to establish. Some of us preferred to use horses which we could handle quietly to reduce the risk. Or was it just an excuse to return to those beloved horses my generation had been reared with?

Every farmer needed turnips, and a constant worry was that the crop would fail either because the weather was too dry to allow the soil to moisten the seed and encourage it to germinate, or in case the dreaded turnip fly (or flea beetle) would eat the tender young growing plant.

At Ballakilmartin in 1940, five acres failed to germinate in an arid May and June, and the ridges were grubbed out, set up again and sown with fresh turnip and kale seed. By then we had missed some of the growing season which is never so good from mid-July onwards.

I found the reference to those worrying days in my 1940 diary, alongside more ominous world news:

June 17th: War situation grave. France today lays down her arms. Britain is left alone to fight Germany and Italy.

July 16: Preparations are made throughout the Island to frustrate any attempt at invasion by Germany. Barricades are being set up on country roads at intervals of three miles. There is one on the White Bridge Hill below our farm gate. Our horses shy at this strange apparition and take lots of persuasion to approach it, even more to pass through it. Billy, the pony, took fright and bolted. I could not hold him but fortunately he galloped home and I found him trembling at the stable door, both he and the float he was pulling unharmed.

Thinning turnips on 'lump work,' the expression for being paid for every 100 yards covered, was a useful source of extra cash for many. It was the practice to pay regular farm staff for thinning turnips after tea at 6pm, while other men and women in the district depended on money the farmers were prepared to pay to get the turnips thinned.

Many of us enjoyed working in the fields on sunny summer evenings, and I always preferred thinning to docking turnips. The workers usually crawled through the ridges with sacks tied around their knees to protect them. Just a few used a hand-held hoe, and walked up and down the ridges.

From our farm account book I find that my uncle was paying 4d. per 100 yards in 1940, but by 1947 the rate had trebled to 1/-. I commented that few people were looking for work on farms by then, partly because returning servicemen wanted something better out of life. I wrote: 'It is just like after the First

Making hay with a pick-up baler, a revolution at the time in 1952, but soon to replace collecting loose hay with a pitchfork. The technique was being demonstrated before farmers who looked on in disbelief at Knockaloe Experimental Farm, operated by the Department (then Board) of Agriculture with George Howie as farm director.

World War when the popular song, "How're you gonna keep 'em down on the farm, after they've seen Paree?" reflected a similar situation.'

In due course we grew fewer turnips and more kale, a leafy plant of the cabbage family, to feed the livestock on our own farm. Kale did not need thinning, and while at first we cut and carted a daily load for the milking cows, we soon adopted a new technique of allowing the cows to graze it for a couple of hours themselves. To stop them spoiling what they could not eat in one meal the grazing was controlled by an electric fence which was moved daily; cows soon came to respect the shock they received from an electric pulse passing through the wire!

Feeding 30 cows in this fashion over 20 winters, until we stopped selling milk in 1985, generated enough cash with a few other additions to pay off the mortgage my wife and I had inherited after my uncle bought the farm a year before he died in 1966.

It was hard work producing milk in buildings designed for the days when labour was cheap and plentiful. At peak output of milk it entailed four hours' milking every day with a bucket machine, on top of the rest of the farm work.

Manx farmers were, and still are, skilled at making hay whether or not the sun shines. In a climate such as ours it means making use of every hour of sun to turn green grass into palatable hay which will keep safely in store without heating. Hay was the complementary feed for turnips until silage replaced both.

Most hay was handled in loose form, prior to the introduction in the 1950s of baling machines which could pick it up from the ground and deliver it in a neat package. A lot of sweat was lost handling it with pitchforks. It had to be turned in the swathe cut by a horse or tractor-drawn reaper, made into small mounds called rucks and after a week or two in the field loaded on carts or trailers for transport to the stacks in the haggart.

'Keep plenty of middle in her,' was the advice to a youngster building loads of hay which he would carry to the stack. A well-settled ruck could be dragged home from the field by a horse once a rope had been passed around its base, although some rucks tumbled over if care had not been taken. Dragging rucks to the stack, whether in field or haggart, was labour-saving in loading carts but not too popular with the men forking onto the stack. With a cart load you had much more height and less lifting.

I earned my first day's wages leading a horse as it dragged in rucks of hay. I would be around 12 at the time, and was paid 6d. one Saturday during the hay harvest. I put it towards saving for my first bicycle, a brand new Vindec costing £3, which two years later I bought from King's shop on Prospect Hill at the end of Athol Street in Douglas.

I learned that day the secret of getting a ruck of hay to travel over rough ground without capsizing. You placed the rope carefully around the base of the ruck, put your full weight on the ruck by lying on the side opposite the direction of movement and coaxing the horse to move gently, and, once the ruck was moving, you raced to the horse's head to grab the bridle and continue the journey home.

But soon that, and many more country skills, would be forgotten with the arrival of that wonderful invention, the pick-up baler.

20

SILAGE OR HAY?

Our friends tease my wife and me that in 50 years of marriage we have had no family – yet! The same can be said about making silage on our farm. I have never made silage, but I was one of the first farm workers in the Island to feed silage to cows. And more than that, I took it to them by horse and cart. It was a true meeting of the old and new worlds in that winter of 1938-39.

My family had just moved from Ballabeg Farm to Ballakilmartin. Across the road at Bibaloe Beg, Tom Kniveton and his sons Clifford and Norman were pioneers of silage-making. They and the Cunningham family at Ellerslie Farm, Crosby, were making silage when every other Manx farmer still depended on growing turnips and hay to feed their animals in winter.

The Knivetons used cereals to make into silage, while today's farmers rely mainly on grass. They cut the crop with a binder which formed it into sheaves, which they forked in green form onto carts or trailers and carried to tower silos. There the sheaves were thrown into a hopper, from which a cutter and blower blew it into the silo. Today's farmers pick up the grass with a machine called a forage harvester, which is designed to drop the material into a trailer travelling alongside.

Tom Kniveton had a surplus of silage in the early months of 1939. He offered some to my uncle as we were short of cattle feed on our new farm. I was sent with a horse and cart to fetch several loads. Litttle did I realise that I was bridging that gap between the old and the new in Manx agriculture.

'A flash in the pan. Well-made hay smells good, silage looks putrid and stinks,' the majority of Manx farmers said. But they reckoned without the final judge, the cow. She relished silage, and gave gallons of milk when fed on it. So there was I in 1939 forking silage with a *graip* onto a stiff cart and leading the horse to our own farm, hoping that I would not meet a neighbour ready to ridicule the idea of feeding silage to cows.

I wish I could boast that because the cows produced more milk and meat when fed silage, we changed our farming methods. But for various reasons this did not happen. On April 10th 1939 I carted my last load of silage, and next season I was back docking turnips.

But other farmers had different ideas, and now at the turn of the new century around 10,000 acres of grass have been turned into silage. 'I can sleep at nights now that I make silage. The rain can beat on my bedroom window, and I am not worried about the hay being ruined in the field', a well-known and successful farmer once told me.

Sixty years ago most farmers still scoffed at the suggestion that silage could replace the hay and turnips grown on every Manx farm. Yet conventional ways of feeding cattle in winter were time-consuming

George Howie supervising threshing at Knockaloe. He was keen to encourage the introduction of silage and in 1961 embarked upon a tour of the Island with a member of the Cheshire Agricultural Executive promoting the use of silage.

were light due to an exceptionally dry May – something in the old saying 'Rain in May brings on the hay', then? Indeed hay was so scarce that the Manx Government, its wartime love of control lingering on, fixed the selling price of hay at £12 per ton. This prevented those with plenty from profiteering, and ensure that those without any could afford some.

Gathering grass for winter feed was again being studied closely during a Young Farmers' educational tour to Scotland in June 1949, but this time the party was enamoured by the new-style pick-up balers which took much of the manual labour out of haymaking. I commented in my journal: 'This machine could mean a renewed interest in hay and turn farmers away from adopting silage. Scottish farmers still have great faith in hay, some of it made by curing grass on tall wooden tripods in the field, but personally I think this is a step too far to go to obtain top quality material. They like turnips too and we saw some magnificent crops of both.'

We talked about silage in 1950, but there were other things on our minds, including the need to rid the Island of the bovine tuberculosis which was killing both humans and cows. On May 11th the Board of Agriculture declared the south of the Island an eradication area; only cattle tested clear of the dreaded disease were allowed south of Douglas.

It was the year when the first Christmas fatstock shows were held following all the wartime controls. At Hollantide 1950 no fewer than 17 farm auctions were held, as well as the three weekly marts, and the countryside buzzed with activity.

in terms of growing the crops and transporting them to the buildings where the animals were housed. In 1947 a party of us Manx Young Farmers watched grass being dried in a huge plant in Cumbria. We would come home and tell the Manx Government that drying grass and turning it into a cube ready for feeding to cows was the answer. Then someone pointed out the cost of the operation and we fell silent; the price of milk could not justify it.

A year later, in July 1948, I wrote that hay crops

90

Those of us driving horses every day opposed Tynwald's bid to prohibit by law the docking of horses' tails. I protested: 'Whoever wants this has never worked a horse in his life in a farm situation, where the long scutch of hair in a horse's natural state can become entangled in following implements such as harrows and, even worse, a reaping machine. When this happens it is sheer cruelty and dangerous to man and horse. As I interpret the proposed law, the old practice of stumping the root of the tail will no longer be allowed, with the result that there will be a lot more time taken in trimming the tail to a safe length.'

I asked my MHK in Middle what it all meant, and he said that it was no use asking him because he hardly knew one end of a horse from the other! But with a general election in November he was anxious to please the majority of voters, and they were against docking horses' tails. That's politics in the Isle of Man for you.

George Howie, ploughing a lonely furrow as the government's only agricultural

As early as 1952, Manx farmers were being encouraged to make silage, picking up the grass with a machine called a Silorator, here seen working at Knockaloe Experimental Farm.

organiser, was keen to encourage the introduction of silage, and in April 1961 he took W. A. C. Carr from the Cheshire Agricultural Executive on a speaking tour of the Island during which he addressed four public meetings.

'Silage should be the mainstay of self-sufficiency on the farm,' Mr. Carr told Manx farmers. '90% of Cheshire farmers depend on it for winter feed. Many have cut out completely the risky business of haymaking with its reliance on fine weather.'

But he warned that a farmer needed to learn a new technique and obtain suitable machinery capable of

gathering green grass. And he must be prepared to fertilise his grass fields to obtain enough material to fill a pit.

By 1956 the Board of Agriculture was putting into practice what agricultural scientists had advised. On June 7th that year, Tom Moore came from the Northern Ireland ministry to set up a demonstration at the Knockaloe Experimental Farm. Two types of collecting grass for silage were used before a large crowd of spectators, many ready to condemn this new-fangled practice, but some at least anxious to swap the labour of turnips and hay for something easier.

The more conventional system was a machine called a silorator which cost the Board £85, and which cut, chopped and blew the grass into an accompanying trailer drawn by a tractor. The second method involved a machine a farmer might already have in use, a pick-up baler for hay and straw. The bales of green grass were lifted by two men (and, boy, were they heavy!) onto a trailer for transport to an earth pit. There were no tractor loaders available in 1956. At the pit the bales had to be pressed tightly together by two or three men to exclude the air which could ruin the silage.

Mr. Moore told his hearers, believers and non-believers alike, that good grass made into silage was the cheapest and most satisfying food for cattle. Purchased meals and nuts were seven times more expensive. In two days as much silage could be made as in the fortnight of gathering hay. 'Where's the sun?' he asked on a dull June day. 'Without it you need lots of effort and patience to extract eight tons of moisture from an acre of grass before it is fit to stack as hay.'

Switching to silage was slow to catch on, however, and it was not until 1984 that more silage than hay was made on Manx farms. Even today hay remains popular, with 6,500 acres being made in the summer of 2001 alongside the 10,000 acres of silage.

Since the 1980s agricultural advisers on the Island have helped to spread the silage gospel, particularly John Bregazzi, John Harris, Robin Allan, Alan Rutherford, Dudley Peck and Caroline Perry. In 1974 Mike Godfrey, who grew vast acres of silage at Ellerslie Farm, Crosby, donated a cup to be awarded annually to the Island's best silage-maker. It was won that year by Dick Callin, then farming at Ballagyr, Peel.

The late Gerald Moore of Cooil Roi Farm, Lonan, was the second winner of the prestigious Ellerslie trophy. The Board of Agriculture continued to promote the competition until in 1978 the Manx Grassland Society was formed, to encourage good farming and continue searching for the best silage maker each year.

The 2001 competition was one of the few farming events to beat the foot-and-mouth shutdown – by just one month – when it was held in January. John Caley took Lheakerrow Farm in Andreas to its eighth success, establishing the most wins ever, a feat accomplished by him and his mother Jean in the annual test of making and using silage.

Over the years since 1974 these winners can be justifiably proud to have had their names inscribed on the Ellerslie Trophy as the best on the Island in silage production. Hubert Kermeen, Ballacraine, St. John's; Sidney and Teddy Corrin, Ballaglonney, Santon; John Kennaugh, Ballawillyn, St. John's; the late Dougie Duggan, Ballavell, Ballasalla (twice); Bernard Callow, Ballaherd, Bride; John and David Huyton, Grenaby Farm, Bride; Steve Martin, Knock-e-Dhooney, Andreas; Keith Teare, Kerrowgarrow, Greeba; John Crellin, Gilcaugh Farm, Andreas (four times); Paul Fargher, Ballawanton, Andreas and Baldromma Farms, Lonan (twice) and Howard Quayle, Ballavitchel, Crosby.

Silage production has become highly technical, and a farmer has to learn the meaning of such terms as energy, digestibility, crude protein, modified fibre, dry matter, volatile fatty acids and amino acid nitrogen among others. It is a far cry from when we were told that turnips contained 97% water (but what water!), and little else of nutritional value.

The humble turnip and hard-won hay helped the farmer feed the nation for centuries, and long before anyone had heard the word silage.

21
A COLOURFUL HISTORY

The history of agricultural societies in the Isle of Man goes back to 1800, when the Manks Agricultural Society was formed as a branch of the Workington Agricultural Society through the efforts of John Christian Curwen the only person ever to have sat in both the House of Commons and the House of Keys. It received scant support from farmers who regarded it as a precursor of more crippling taxation, and they were loath to exhibit their animals because they believed it might reveal assets the tax man did not know about. The last show was held in Athol Street, Douglas on October 12th 1812, instead of the planned venue of St. John's. The bad state of the roads coupled with a wet summer had made country travel difficult.

There was a gap of almost 30 years before a second society was formed. The new Isle of Man Agricultural Society held its first show in Duke's Yard in Lord Street, Douglas, on Hollantide Fair Day 1841.

It took more than a day's droving to move cattle, sheep and pigs to Douglas from some outlying farms. The best bulls came from Edward Faulder of Ellerslie Farm, Crosby, William Farrant, Jurby and William Teare, Ballawhane, Andreas, and the winning cows from Thomas Auchen in Castletown and John Blythe of Ronaldsway.

The aim of the second agricultural society was to take its show to the people, and it was staged at the Green in Ramsey in 1842 and at Scarlett near Castletown in 1843. The fourth show, at the lake by the harbour in Peel in July 1844, was hit by bad weather, with heavy rain and strong westerly winds deterring people from attending. As a result the society found itself in serious financial difficulty.

But by then there were already murmurs that the society was only there to benefit the rich and injure the poor. The fact that 80 of the gentry sat down to a sumptuous meal after each show while those less fortunate began the long trek home on foot, often driving or leading animals, did not encourage support.

In 1845 the society's fourth show in Braaid's Yard, Douglas, on October 21st proved to be its last. Entries were down, not least because its president E. M. Gawne of Kentraugh, Castletown, sent a horseman to recall his cattle when they were already being walked towards Douglas. Apparently he had heard that morning that a disease the Manx called the murrain was spreading throughout the Island's cattle and he had no wish for his animals to come into contact with it.

The society claimed that it had at least improved standards in Manx agriculture. Formerly flour had had to be imported from Liverpool to feed the people, but by 1843 the trade had flowed the other way, with wheat to the value of £500 and tons of potatoes being exported after the needs of the Island had been met. In an impassioned appeal to save the society Samuel

Rogers, the secretary, said: 'It's true that men of wealth have come forward to nobly support our funds, but we want the support of the small farmers – the shillings and half crowns of the lower orders as well as the five and ten pounds of the more wealthy.' When they did not respond the second agricultural society petered out.

By 1858 farming was developing along more scientific lines, and in the Manx countryside there were people who considered that local agriculture was being left behind in the progress made elsewhere in crop and livestock production. A group of enthusiasts met in Douglas in March 1858 to form the third agricultural society, which survives to this day. It launched a show in the Nunnery grounds on September 30th, with Deemster Drinkwater from Ballaughton, Braddan, as president.

The winning exhibit was a red and white bull called Sultan, shown by Evan Gell of Whitehouse Farm, Kirk Michael. The *Manx Sun* reported that 'not everyone agreed with the judge and many observers thought that the bull belonging to Mr. Ormerod of Ballawhane, Andreas, placed third, was the best'. Livestock judging was then, as now, in the eye of the beholder.

The choice of the Nunnery did not escape the notice of the *Mona's Herald* reporter who, contemplating the scene with some distaste, mused 'Should St. Bridget, the lady paramount of this domain, descend from glory or ascend from purgatory on the show day, what would be her emotions to see hundreds of worldly-minded men, showy women, stallions rampant, bulls pawing up the consecrated ground and sleepy pigs too fat to keep their eyes open?'

But the pattern was set for regular summer shows which have continued every year since, except in 1866, during the two World Wars, and in 2001 as an anti-foot-and-mouth precaution. The shows alternated between Douglas and Ramsey and became so popular that from 1879 to 1881 two were held each year, organised by separate North and South committees in their own districts. In 1886 the society promoted its first Christmas fatstock show in Kelly's Yard, Douglas.

The summer show visited Castletown on only four occasions, the last time in 1893. At stormy meetings in Douglas, Southside farmers and tradesmen pleaded for its return 'over the bridge', but consistently lost on a vote. Eventually they resigned from the council and formed their own Southern District Agricultural Society, to begin annual shows with the first at Billown, Ballasalla, in 1914.

The Isle of Man Agricultural Society's shows have always reflected the march of mechanisation. The most exciting development was the invention of the self-binder which not only cut the corn but delivered it in a neat sheaf tied by twine. It appeared at shows in the 1870s alongside improved horse-drawn ploughs and better butter churns invariably sold out on the field.

Hurdle-jumping, a forerunner of today's extensive equestrian section, was a popular spectacle for many years. And from its inception the Society undertook 'to reward servants of both sexes in husbandry with unblemished characters for the longest period in their respective services'; it still presents farm workers with long service awards.

In 1906 the Society deviated from its usual role of promoting exhibitions of livestock and produce to plant 24,822 trees on Slieu Whallian, at a labour cost of £80, in the days before the Manx Government assumed responsibility for forestry.

Both agricultural societies and the Isle of Man Farmers' Club (now Isle of Man Farmers' Limited) were spokesmen for farming in the political and marketing arena, particularly at government level, until specialist organisations, the Agricultural Marketing Society, in 1934, and the Manx National Farmers' Union, in 1946, replaced them.

In 1951, through the efforts of its president Ramsey Johnson, the Isle of Man Agricultural Society received permission from King George VI to use the title Royal

Manx; this brought it into line with the national organisations of England, Scotland, Wales and Ulster.

When tourism was still in its heyday, the Isle of Man (now Royal Manx) show was one of the season's biggest attractions. It was always held on the Thursday of August Bank Holiday week, when arrivals of holidaymakers were at their peak. Huge crowds would walk out from Douglas to the Nunnery Park or catch trains and buses to Ramsey for the shows which alternated between the two locations each year. But eventually their popularity led to the shows outgrowing both sites.

The last show on the Lezayre playing fields took place in 1972, and two years later Staward Farm at Sulby was used as the northern site for the first time. The Douglas show moved from the Nunnery to the King George V Park in 1961, but by 1990 the park and adjoining Bowl were needed for the new National Sports Centre. The Manx Government offered a venue at St. John's, but the Society decided to adopt Staward Farm at Sulby on a permanent basis and entered into a 20-year lease with the owners.

The last show at the King George V Park, in 1989, coincided with the first visit by a member of the British royal family, and it was with great pride that members welcomed Queen Elizabeth and Prince Philip. To accord with their programme the show was switched to a Monday and Tuesday from its time-honoured slot with Thursday as the main exhibition day. In 1998, however, the Thursday tradition was abandoned in favour of a weekend show, with opening on Friday and Saturday as the main livestock day. Without adequate housing, there are no facilities to keep animals overnight for the duration of the show.

Despite a recession in agriculture and fewer people engaged in farming, the Royal Manx Annual Summer Show seems set to stay as one of the major events of the year.

(Left) R. G. Shimmin's Ransomes, Sims and Jeffries engine and mill with Eddie Brew as engine driver at Ballakilmurray, near Peel, in the 1940s, threshing for Messrs Killey.
(Below) Robert Bruce from Ramsey used this outfit comprising Wallis and Stevens steam engine, Ruston threshing mill and baler on farms in the north of the Island.

(Photos: Stephen Carter)

(Below inset) Field Marshall diesel tractors replaced steam engines as motive power for threshing mills during miners' strikes in the UK after the war when coal became scarce. This outfit, owned by Peter Howe of Ballagunnell, Andreas revives threshing scenes of the 1950s at the 2002 Royal Manx Agricultural Show at Sulby.

(Photo: Ian Quayle)

FLYING MAN AT RAMSEY SHOW!

Thousands of people thronged the agricultural showground, yet within 10 minutes it was almost empty. But why? It was 1912 and the Isle of Man Agricultural Show was being held outside Ramsey in the shadow of the battlefield of Sky Hill, but another battle also overshadowed the day.

This was against the threat of foot-and-mouth disease. 'There is not a single case of the disease in the Island', stated the Mona's Herald of August 14th, 'but with farmers present from England and Ireland where the present outbreak originated it would not be a matter of wonder if the farmers kept their valuable stock at home.'

There were 132 cattle, 160 horses, 83 sheep and six pigs there, but it was nothing to do with fears about animal disease which caused the rapid evacuation of the busy show field.

The grand parade, always the leading feature of a Manx agricultural show, was reaching its expected climax when some eagle-eyed spectators spotted a speck in the sky. 'A flying man!', they shouted, and pointed to him.

There, 3,000 feet above the Albert Tower, was a man travelling at one mile a minute and heading towards them. It was the pioneer aviator, Gustave Hamel, piloting his primitive plane on a journey from Douglas to Ramsey.

An 80-year-old man exclaimed, 'I see him. I see the flying man. I never hoped to see the like. Oh dear me!' according to the Mona's Herald. 'Then he became speechless in rapt gaze of the man earthly who was to him, perhaps, a vision of angels.'

Mr. Hamel landed his wonderful machine in a field adjoining the show, and there was an immediate 'helter skelter' from the showfield to see the man and his flying apparatus. A paygate was hurriedly set up and 6d. per person charged, but after the first stream paid their money the rush was so great that the pay table was overturned. All sorts, it was reported, overwhelmed the stewards – gentlemen, farm hands, old women and young ladies – and for half an hour Mr. Hamel signed autographs.

He had brought a letter from Alderman Joughin, Mayor of Douglas, for the chairman of Ramsey Town Commissioners to establish the first post by air. People kept pouring in to witness the take off, or 'ascent' as the newspaper called it. They described it as the most marvellous sight of their lives.

Hamel circled the show field several times to loud cheering before heading for Douglas, which he expected to reach in 12 minutes after following the sea coast for 15 miles.

Then the crowd turned back to acclaim the winners. Among them was a Clydesdale mare shown by John Cowin of Ballachrink, Onchan, who was described by the Mona's Herald reporter as the youngest-looking old farmer on the Island; 'We think that his age is about 85.' Today John Cowin still has descendants on the Island engaged in agriculture.

(I am indebted to Braddan farmer and author Hampton Creer for much of this information)

22
THE 'WILD WEST' RUSTLERS

In the 1850s the agricultural revolution which would lead to an improvement in food production reached the Isle of Man. Subsistence farming, where people grew their own food or bought it from neighbours with money or barter, gave way to an agricultural industry supplying the needs of the community.

But at that time Manx farmers were not so much concerned with adopting more scientific methods as with safeguarding their animals and crops from theft. A spirit of lawlessness akin to that ruling in the Wild West of America was abroad in the Manx countryside, although there was no law of the gun. No cow, no sheep, no hen was safe from rustlers looking for easy living, and highway robbery of those travelling on foot or in horse drawn vehicles was rife. Sheep-stealing and hen roost robberies were the main concern, and early records of the Agricultural Society indicate that they were subjects under frequent discussion.

The day had passed when men (and women) were hung or transported to a distant land for the theft of a sheep, and by 1869 the Manx Government was even turning a blind eye on such crimes.

On January 13th 1869 members of the Isle of Man Farmers' Club met in the British Hotel, Douglas 'to consider what might be advisable to suppress the agricultural thefts so prevalent throughout the island'. It was claimed at the meeting that the police, and farmers themselves, were reluctant to report thefts because they generally knew who committed them and often the culprit was a friend, a neighbour or a relative.

Peter Cadman of Howstrake Farm, Onchan, called for action. A new Sheep Stealing Prevention Association within the club was set up, and Mr. Cadman was elected chairman. He was an ancestor of the Quayle family of Glenlough Farm near Union Mills, and they still have his handwritten records. They show that a list of 243 sheep known to have disappeared off lowland and hill was submitted to the first meeting. Also under consideration were dozens of 'hen roost robberies.'

Henry Sneddon, farming at Pulrose Farm in Braddan, reported that one farmer in his district had had some fowls taken and informed the police. But they had done nothing, and over two following nights the thieves had returned and cleared his roost of every hen. T. J. Taubman complained that it was no use talking to the rural police: 'I got a coroner and a policeman and went to search for a missing goose and found it half way up a chimney. I took the persons to Ramsey and kept them in the lock up for 24 hours when they were released without charge!'

The situation reached a climax when a man who 'had seen the light' at a Methodist revival in Peel and Dalby repented his sins and confessed that he and a partner had stolen 90 sheep from Mr. Dodd, who farmed at Ballacallin in Patrick.

The man, seeking to avoid eternal damnation and hell fire in days when Anglicans and Methodists did battle against each other, went on to tell the Methodists that one of his best customers was the vicar of Patrick, who enjoyed a dinner of mutton many times a week!

In the following months more owners of lost sheep came forward. Philip Quayle of Balleigh, Michael, was 15 short, John Brook, Druidale, 13, and S. H. Harrison had 22 missing from fields in German parish. Butchers in Braddan found 14 had gone from land where they kept sheep prior to slaughter.

Mr. Cadman told a meeting: 'It has been found the best policeman is an intelligent Irishman who does not know the locals.' To which Mr. Taubman called out, 'It is no use having either Scotsmen or Irishmen here. We need an honest Englishman!'

The Chief Constable, George Goldie, defended his force by declaring that the owners of sheep suspected stolen left it too late before telling his men, and by then the trail had gone cold. He detailed three cases which had been investigated. Edward Farrant had reported the loss of one sheep. Constable Kermode and the Coroner had searched every suspicious house in Ramsey and Lezayre and found nothing. Mr. Farrant expressed himself satisfied with the inquiries.

In the second case a man named Cowin was found with stolen mutton in his possession. The coroner seized the meat but lost the man. Constable Kermode, an astute officer, followed Cowin to Douglas and, with the help of Sergeant Hollinrake and Constable Callow, took him off the Silloth steamer a few minutes before it sailed. Cowin was committed to gaol.

A Mr. Brook gave information of sheep being stolen. This led to a cart being followed by police into Douglas, where a quantity of 'warm meat' was recovered.

Some progress was being made in scaring off the thieves, but Captain Penketh complained that under Manx law the police had no power to arrest men, even when they were known to be sheep stealers. Mutton, geese and fowl were offered for sale in Douglas market. No one asked where they came from.

Captain Goldie proposed to a meeting in November 1869 that the Governor, Sir Henry Loch, should be asked to appoint extra policemen but that as he was not expected to return to the Island for another six or seven weeks His Excellency should issue an order from London.

In time more rural police patrolled the countryside and co.-operated with vigilantes operating in bands in the parishes. The Governor returned to the Island and with the Attorney General met farmers and flockmasters, advising them to adopt a voluntary system of earmarking sheep for easy identification. Butchers had to obtain licences before they could set up in business and were obliged to keep records of all animals they handled.

Trespassing laws were enforced; in 1871 William Brew, suspected of sheep stealing, was acquitted of the charge but gaoled for trespass. In August that year 53 witnesses were called to an inquiry by a trespass jury accusing Thomas Gawne of Laurel Bank in German of damage to goods and property. The jury of Charles Radcliffe, Daniel Sheard, Thomas Shimmin and Thomas Radcliffe found the case unproven, although popular opinion did not agree.

However law and order were improving, and the efforts of the Sheep Stealing Prevention Association had drawn attention to the need for action. It met on February 23rd 1873, but there are no records of minutes after that date or evidence that the committee was ever convened again.

It was not only the meat from a sheep that was valuable. Wool commanded such a good price that in 1864 the *Mona's Herald* declared that by yielding a fleece in May or June a sheep would pay for its keep for a whole year. Hampton Creer says that in his study of farming records in the 1600s and 1700s he found wool to be the most expensive commodity on the farm, selling in pounds sterling compared with shillings and pence for other products.

Machines were being introduced to agriculture, not least the coal-fired steam engine which supplied power, especially for threshing the corn. The same Edward Farrant from Ballamoar, Jurby, who was concerned about sheep stealing brought the first steam threshing outfit to the Island.

Two farmers in the north of the Island, Mr. Allan and Mr. McWhannell, identified an opening for business, and on December 21st 1864 announced in the local press that their travelling threshing and winnowing machines would be available for hire at a charge of 25/- per day. They assured farmers that the outfit would pass through an ordinary cart gateway, a matter of concern then with new implements as it was to be the next century, when combine harvesters were found to be too wide to enter many fields and hedges had to be demolished. Allan and McWhannell's service marked the start of the 'mill days', a feature of Manx farm life until the 1960s.

A couple of years earlier, in September 1862, the Isle of Man Agricultural Society had held a trial for the new-fangled reaping machines at Ballagarey, Marown. Six machines, either made locally or imported, were timed cutting a similar area of oats. The reapers were pulled by a single horse or by a pair walking abreast. The judges, Samuel Broadbent and Henry Siddons, declared that in their opinion the machines could not be equalled by sickle or scythe.

They awarded the first prize of £5 to a reaper made by Cain & Nicklin of Douglas. Second prize of £3 went to Lewin & Kissack of Crosby, and £2 to James Kelly, address unknown.

By this time more people were learning to read, and in August 1867 the *Mona's Herald* announced that it had appointed 'a gentleman' to compile a weekly agricultural calendar. He was to be in complete charge of a new department capable of answering any queries on practical agriculture and would be writing articles. The editor asked for themes for him to comment upon.

His first subject emphasised the advantage of spreading lime on the land as a means of totally eradicating the wire worm which ate the roots of growing plants. The lengthy article claimed that lime improved the growth of crops, but made no mention of the main characteristic for which it is valued today, of balancing the acidity and alkalinity of soils. Probably this factor was nor realised in those days, and there was a mystery about its beneficial effect.

Lime was obtained from the limestone found in the south of the Island. After quarrying and burning it was carried by boats and shovelled overboard onto the beaches where farmers picked it up with horses and carts. Farmers in the north of the Island also needed lime, but another organisation, the Northern Farmers' Club, found it cheaper and more convenient to bring supplies from England through the port of Whitehaven.

The need for manuring crops was increasingly appreciated and 'patent' manures were already imported on a small scale, but in 1874 the Isle of Man Patent Manure Company Ltd. was founded with a capital of £15,000 in £1 shares to manufacture manures 'to replace inferior and doubtful manures now being commonly pawned upon the agriculturalists of the Island'.

Captain R. Penketh from Hampton Court, Port Soderick, was again to the fore as chairman, together with Samuel Broadbent, Bibaloe, Onchan, Frank Twigg, Bishopscourt, Michael, Thomas Faragher, Derbyhaven, Edward Crellin, The Friary, Arbory and William and Thomas Kelly of Douglas. Company Secretary was Thomas Bawden of Market Place, Douglas.

23
MUCH BINDING ON THE FARM

The idea of one man driving three horses and doing the work of a gang of 10 or more men, women and children, could still be a matter of wonderment in my youth in the harvest field.

There were plenty of people around in the 1920s and 1930s who remembered the harvest being gathered by men cutting corn with a scythe or sickle, while others together with women collected the corn into sheaves, and every available child was expected to do some of the lighter work. But the invention of a machine which could cut, bind and deliver a sheaf as fast as a horse could walk revolutionised farming from the time of its invention by Cyrus McCormick in the USA in 1878. Before the 19th century ended every Manx farm had its self-binder, and until we bought our first tractor in 1943 it was the biggest and most valuable machine on the farm.

My first recollection of a binder was in the harvest of 1926, when as a young boy newly arrived in the Island from the smoky cotton town of Burnley I found the life I was to love in a cornfield adjoining Cronkbourne Village. The smell of the corn mingling with the scent of flowers and herbs in the hedgerows, the peace – apart from the subdued clatter of the binder or the snort of a horse – the realisation of being involved in an annual miracle of nature, are all memories no one who knew them will ever forget.

Harold Gale, who farmed at Ballacowle near Bride Church, told me that his father brought one of the first binders to the Isle of Man in the 1890s. It was a Plano by make, manufactured in the USA, and it arrived on the farm in a wooden packing crate and was assembled by a travelling mechanic.

Soon, local agricultural merchants began selling binders of various makes. Corlett Sons & Cowley brought in Massey Harris, Charles H. Teare of Castletown the Hornsby, and Clague & Craine of Ridgeway Street, Douglas, the Albion. Their prices were very competitive; most of them quoted at £56 for a model which could cut a five foot swathe at a time.

T. W. Kelly, also in Ridgeway Street, Douglas, was agent for the International Harvester Company, which had been formed by the merger of two firms of implement manufacturers, McCormick & Deering. The new company continued to make two binders, which turned out to be identical in every respect except colour. They called one McCormick and painted it red; the other Deering appeared in blue livery. The only difference was £2 in price, the McCormick being the dearer. According to legend, most Manx farmers bought the McCormick because as it was dearer they thought it must be better. This story is often told to sales people on training courses as a example of the gullibility of the buying public!

With the coming of the binder came a new necessity, that of 'cutting roads' around each corn field. One swathe of the scythe was cut to enable the horses – generally two instead of three in the opening round –

101

My uncle, Jim McCubbin, driving our new Nuffield tractor pulling an Albion binder to cut oats in 1953.

Albert Sayle, showed me his way and I succeeded immediately. It transpired that my uncle was left-handed and Albert and I were right-handed. It taught me early in life that following *kithaggy*-handed people could lead to problems. *Kithaggy*, incidentally, is Manx for left-handed.

At Ballabeg Farm we had a binder made by Walter A. Wood of Horsham, Sussex. Its agents were two brothers, the Gales on the Quay in Ramsey. One August evening in 1936 we were cutting corn with three horses when the dew descended (or ascended – experts still argue which) rather rapidly. Cutting damp corn put a strain on the three canvasses which carried the corn from the cutter bar to the sheaf board, and one of the canvasses with its wooden lathes split badly, beyond repair. We needed a new one before we could continue the next day.

Early the following morning I was despatched to catch the 7.30am Douglas-to-Ramsey bus at St. Ninian's. The fare, I remember, was 2/- return. In Ramsey I bought a new canvas from the Gale brothers, who I recall wore khaki dust coats as part of their shop livery. I returned from Ramsey, walking home from St. Ninian's, and soon we were ready to start cutting again as the dew dried off the corn.

In 1936 we, like most households, had no motor vehicle of any kind, and the only way to travel was by to travel around the field without trampling and spoiling the crop. Every sheaf, every ear, was valuable and could not be wasted.

I was soon old enough to make bands to bind the sheaves when cutting roads. You took an equal number of stalks of oats – the staple cereal then – in each hand, crossing and twisting them until you had a band almost twice in length of the cut stalks. They were laid on the ground, and one man would lift enough corn in his arms for a sheaf. He then placed his loose sheaf on the band for another man to tie.

But it took me a long time to learn to make a band. My uncle who was trying to teach me became exasperated, cursing my stupidity until one of the men, horse, bicycle, on foot or, in this case, bus. Others, of course, could use the steam or electric trains regularly, but we had a long walk to any station.

Not everyone shared my enthusiasm for the harvest, especially those driven to distraction by the midges and the harvest bugs which burrowed under the skin. None of these worried me, then or now.

Alongside the mechanical revolution there were improvements in farming methods, with crops and animals which made UK and Manx agriculture among the most efficient in the world.

At a time when country members outnumbered town representatives in both Keys and Council, there emerged a faction who believed that the best way to support the Island's chief basic industry was by encouraging farmers to produce more food. Demand was there, both from the permanent population and from the extra mouths to be fed during the booming holiday season.

But it was not the government which provided the funds. Instead it came from a source with no previous connections with the countryside. Henry Bloom Noble, the greatest benefactor the Island has ever known, and whose vast wealth helped to found Noble's Hospital, Noble's Park and Noble's Baths among a host of other projects, left £20,000 for the encouragement of agriculture in the Isle of Man.

Trustees of his will agreed after much deliberation to use the money to establish and maintain an experimental farm. They looked around the Island and decided to buy and reclaim a farm which had been lost to agriculture when it housed 30,000 enemy aliens and their guards during the First World War. The farm was Knockaloe Moar near Patrick Church, extending to 346 acres but totally scarred and derelict.

Knockaloe cost the Manx Government £7,800, and the rest of the £20,000 would be needed to restore the holding to a good state of fertility after 10 years of neglect. It took until 1930 after a full seven-year Manx rotation of crops for the soil to be pronounced 'almost normal'.

With the appointment of George Howie, a canny Scotsman, as agricultural organiser and farm director in 1928, experiments began in growing and harvesting crops and in using the farm as a centre for breeding top class cattle, sheep, pigs and poultry. Herds of Beef Shorthorn and Aberdeen Angus cattle were established, promoting two of Scotland's indigenous breeds in accordance with Mr. Howie's connection with his native country.

Knockaloe's Suffolk sheep flock, founded in 1925, is one of the oldest pedigree flocks in Britain. Large White pigs were bred for a market where almost every Manx farm kept a breeding sow or two. The pedigree breeding programme, with some changes over the years, has progressed further under Mr. Howie's two successors, John Bregazzi from 1964 to 1991 and Dudley Peck since then.

Until artificial insemination removed the need for so many bulls, the Board of Agriculture sent two leading farmers each year on a buying mission to England and Scotland to secure bulls for sale to Manx farms. With individual farmers importing stock, too, the quality of the Island's cattle, sheep and pigs increased dramatically.

It was a far cry from the days when the Isle of Man depended on native animals of indiscriminate origin. Island cows, for instance, were very small in stature; proof of that lies in the first cowshed erected at Ballakilmartin with its narrow and short stalls for eight milking cows. The Island also had a breed of roving wild pigs or 'purrs', covered in bristles, but some were domesticated, especially by cottage dwellers who kept a pig to eat household scraps and fatten to provide pork and bacon.

Loaghtan sheep are the only survivors of our native livestock. They are now enjoying a boom because of the valuable genes they possess, their gamey eating flavour, unique wool and novelty value. In days past their commercial value could not compare with that of the improved British breeds and they survived only through the enthusiasm of a few people 40 years ago.

The year 1932 was the starting point for much of the advisory work initiated by George Howie. He wrote an advisory leaflet, the first of many circulated to farmers, entitled 'Rations for dairy cows with special regard to the utilisation of oats'. It recommended the right quantities of the only feed grown on farms at the time, turnips (extending to 5,000 acres), oats (called corn in the Isle of Man) of which there were 15,000 acres, hay and straw.

The daily cost of feeding for an adult cow ranged from 6d. to 10d., the latter for a cow in milk. 'I will be pleased to prepare rations to utilise other feeding stuffs, home grown or purchased which Manx farmers may have on hand,' offered Mr Howie.

The turnips fed 24,000 cattle in winter – 32,000 today – with some for the 75,000 sheep (more than double that number graze the Isle of Man now). On our own farm we grew almost 10 acres of turnips, mostly for stock food but with the best of the crop exported in bags to the Liverpool vegetable market. In 1940 the turnip field at Ballakilmartin was the one running parallel with the White Bridge Hill. It is known as the Chapel Field because it contains the ruins of a Primitive Methodist chapel built in 1826 and used until 1902.

In a wet winter the top gateway of the field became water logged and on one occasion Billy Kelly, the cowman, decided to use another route. He led his horse, Prince, with a full load of turnips out of the gate at the bottom of the field and onto the main road which passes our farm entrance. This made haulage for the horse much lighter.

Billy guided Prince home and once there backed the cart into the shed where the turnips were stored. He then went to 'kick the load' – the expression for tipping the stiff cart – and to his astonishment there was not a single turnip in the cart he had so laboriously filled. Perplexed, he retracted his steps with Prince and the empty cart. It was not until he reached the foot of the hill that he found the turnips he had lost.

Billy was deaf, which meant that he did not hear the lads from Onchan Village who crept out of Molly Quirk's Glen to undo the tail board of the cart and let the turnips roll out and down the hill. He picked up the tail board, replaced it, and began to collect the turnips and re-load them, all the while cursing loudly. Devilment like that was not unusual in the countryside and people accepted it; today, of course, it would be labelled vandalism.

To their credit, once the fun was over the lads reappeared and helped Billy gather his load (it would be unfair of me to name the pranksters, who grew up to be respected men still playing a prominent part in community life). 'Did you lose your load, Billy?' they shouted. 'I must have done; thank you for helping me,' he replied, not suspecting why he lost it.

But turnips played a very important part in country life. No child ever went hungry as long as there were some growing in the fields, which they were from August to April. If no one in our gang possessed a penknife, a sharp slate or stone would suffice to trim the skin from the turnip.

24
MORNING MILK & HIGH SPIRITS

Rows of spirit glasses, each containing a tot of rum, used to be lined up on the counters of bars in hotels in Douglas to greet men from the farms making early-morning deliveries of milk with a horse and float. These milkmen would pour a quantity of milk, still warm from the cow, uncooled and unpasteurised, straight into each glass. Holidaymakers out for a walk before breakfast clamoured for this taste of luxury living; they would enjoy it for just one week in the year before returning to the grind of their everyday lives, usually in the industrial north of England.

From the tales told to me by an older generation it seems this custom went on in those heady days following the end of World War One. It may have come to a halt after Tynwald amended the licensing laws to outlaw morning opening of pubs in 1921, but on the other hand the milk-round lads spoke of the back door being left on the latch for them to enter. Perhaps an illicit trade was carried on through the same door? It was rumoured that one or two policemen plodding on foot around the town had a fondness for an early morning rum and milk, too.

Every town, but particularly Douglas, provided a market for farmers delivering their produce by horse and cart. Those farming close to the towns had an advantage in supplying the boarding houses and hotels in the days before motor transport developed after 1945. Outlying farms could not get perishable foods to buyers in time until cooling methods and refrigeration became feasible. The farms near centres of population paid for the privilege, because rents at the time were £3 an acre around Douglas, compared with £2 in Bride or other outlying parishes.

The first attempt to use milk surplus to the needs of the resident population or the holidaymakers came in 1922, when the Isle of Man Dairies established the first factory cheese-making enterprise at Spring Gardens in Douglas. You can't turn a cow's production of milk off as with a tap, and there was often far too much for the liquid market. Cheese was a more attractive proposition than pouring the milk down the drain, a common practice before organised marketing.

Cheese-making had not been widespread on Manx farms, but butter-making took place on most dairy farms. It was hard work, especially for the women who were reckoned to be best at it. Cheese gave a better return because one gallon of milk will make one pound, while it takes two to three gallons for a pound of butter.

Nevertheless good Manx butter sold well even in competition with foreign imports. There are still prizes for handmade butter at the agricultural shows although entries are few nowadays. Two magnificent trophies on offer at the Royal Manx were donated many years ago by Sir Frederick Clucas, Speaker of the House of Keys.

In the past the entrants had to make the butter on the show field, revolving the churn at a steady pace

105

Farmers' wives and daughters at a cheese-making class in Ramsey sometime between 1913 and 1918.

until the milk turned into butter. In 1932, 10 butter makers, men as well as women, competed against each other in a marquee. We don't know who won but here are the 10 who tried: Nancy Sutherland, Bay View Road, Port St. Mary; Vera Corris, 28 Malew Street, Castletown; Phyllis Kelly, Ballanank, Malew; Annie Quirk, Ballachrink, Dalby; Lilla Quirk, Ballalaa, Dalby; Margaret Moughtin, Tynwald Road, Peel; Eddie Kelly, Shenvalley Cottage, Patrick; Robert Penrice, Cooperative House, Market Street, Peel; John Quirk, Gib Lane, Peel; Hilda Cain, Laurel Bank, St. John's.

The judge was a Miss M. McArthur from the West of Scotland College of Agriculture. Dairying and poultry keeping were still important cash-earners on farms and as well as the butter-making competition there were demonstrations of making soft and cream cheese as well as trussing poultry for the oven.

At the time attempts were being made to revive the growing of flax for manufacturing into linen. It had been a useful crop in years past, as the number of ruins of flax mills on the Island confirms. In the depressed 1930s it was seen as an alternative to less profitable crops, the sort of diversification being encouraged today in a similar financial situation.

R. C. (Bertie) Gill was experimenting with flax at Ballavarrey in Andreas and some of his 1932 crop was on display at the show. But although Mr. Gill and others proved that flax could be grown successfully in Manx soils, the Isle of Man could not compete with the

Lady members of the Young Farmers' Clubs at a butter making class in Braddan Church Hall in 1956. From left, Betty Teare, instructress, Marjorie Joughin, Pat Corrin, Nancy Taggart, Glen Clelland, Edith Callin, Kathleen Taggart, Margaret Quayle, Marie Corlett and Laura, wife of the author.

Irish linen industry. As with sugar beet some years later the cost of building processing plants was not justified by the limited supply of the raw material.

The same species of plant which produces flax also provides linseed at a different stage of growth. Linseed can be ground into an oil for industrial use or used as cattle feed, but it has not caught on in a big way in the Island, thankfully for those of us who helped to thresh it during the last war.

It was harvested in sheaves, as with cereals, and threshed to separate the seed from the straw with the travelling mills in winter. Anyone on the board (top) of the mill - there would be three of us, one to cut the twine off the sheaf, another to hand the sheaf to the third, the feeder who dropped it into the revolving drum – would be continually peppered in the face as the linseed shot off the drum, which did not happen when threshing other crops. The answer was to wear goggles or other face protection, but none could be bought during wartime.

Once the risk of wartime gas attacks receded we took our government-issue gas masks and cut them up to make goggles, to be worn not only when threshing linseed but also for other dusty and hazardous jobs. This explains why so few gas masks survive on farms.

In 1932 the Board of Agriculture was conducting egg-laying trials to discover which breed or type of hen laid the most eggs and was the most profitable. A trial began on October 15th, when poultry keepers were invited to enter their flocks in three sections, an open class, another for those with no more than 150 birds, and the third confined to *bona fide* general farms.

Young Farmers' Clubs' wives and daughters were very active in their organisation of cookery classes. Margaret Quayle (nee Lace) is seen here studying recipes.

A year later the trials proved that the ordinary farmyard hen was laying a mere 90 eggs in 365 days. Allowing that a hen should lay one egg every day with a few weeks' rest, this showed that most Manx hens were idle for 275 days every year, which prompted one farmer to declare that if his wife worked so little he would screw her neck. And that precisely was what happened to the hens which did not achieve an accepted target. The trials helped farmers to breed better egg-laying strains of hens, and ten years later a similar trial demonstrated that Manx hens were laying 200 eggs per annum.

It is a pity that this pioneering work was lost when another Board (or by then, Department) of Agriculture in the 1990s sacrificed the Isle of Man's poultry industry on the altar of free trade, under controversial EU rules which many who lost their livelihoods feel could have been legally challenged. As a result the number of laying hens on Manx farms dropped from 120,000 in 1973 to 22,211 in 1997. The blame must go to the Manx Government's neglect of the poultry industry, aided and abetted by a regulation-mad EU and UK politicians like Edwina Currie who started the salmonella witch hunt. Now probably more eggs than ever are consumed on the Island, but most come from sources where hens have to live in conditions Manx farmers would not tolerate.

On 28 September 1985, milk churns were collected from farms by the Isle of Man Milk Marketing Association for the last time. Dave Fisher and Ernie Radcliffe, employees of the Association, are seen here with the author at Ballakilmartin on the very last churn collection before road tankers took over.

In 1949, to take a year at random, egg sales were an important part of a farm's economy, alongside revenue from milk, beef, lamb, wood, potatoes, vegetables and table poultry. There was money, too, from the sale of oats not needed on the farm for feeding to horses, cattle, sheep and poultry. With a little of everything we were cushioned from losses on any one particular commodity. Some of the food we grew we ate ourselves, and probably at no time in history were families more self sufficient. The family farm employing men and women from the surrounding district seemed likely to continue for ever.

I even grew tobacco for my newly-acquired habit of smoking a pipe. At first this was to impress the girls because did their heroes in the pictures we went to at least once a week not look dashing brandishing a pipe? Of course, I was soon addicted to tobacco and I smoked a pipe for 40 years. Why buy it when I could grow it?

In 1949 I sent to an address in Somerset for one dozen Havana tobacco plants at a cost of 7/-. They duly arrived and I transplanted them into the farm garden, where they flourished. I had enough leaves to keep me in tobacco for a year. But I found growing tobacco easy, curing it for an enjoyable smoke much harder. I was told to soak the leaves in rum, but I knew that bringing a bottle to the farm would definitely not

Left to right: Nancy Taggart, Glen Clelland and Pat Corrin being briefed in the finer arts of butter making by instructress Betty Teare, far left.

be allowed; the only drink ever seen in our house was port wine at Christmas. I tried to cure the leaves, but when I smoked them they tasted foul and smelled horrible. They were driving away the girls I was trying to attract, so I went back to Monty Fargher's shop in Onchan to buy Battleaxe, Condor and St. Bruno.

The women on the farm were expected to look after the poultry, except at Christmas when the men helped with the plucking of turkeys, geese, ducks and chickens and with that unsavoury job, cleaning out the hen house.

The poultry were mostly free range, perching everywhere, even on trees on wild wet winter nights, silly creatures, but some of us were trying the new system of keeping laying hens in deep litter. This involved scattering layers of straw in a shed or loose box and keeping the hens indoors at all times.

We soon discovered which hens were laying, and those which were not were speedily returned to the rest of the flock roaming the fields and farmyard. The report on the egg-laying experiments was studied by my aunt, who had college qualifications in poultry-keeping as well as dairying.

We were advised on the breeds best to produce eggs, and each spring we brought in day-old chicks from UK hatcheries because Knockaloe could not meet the demand. In spring, too, we had to look ahead to Christmas when there would be a market for table birds of all domestic species, even in wartime. Here are a couple of extracts from my diary of 1942:

April 22nd: Hen set on eight turkey eggs. We purchased two dozen turkey eggs from Mrs. Corrin, Creggan Moar, Dalby, at 2/- per egg. The turkeys out of the eggs will be reared for the Christmas trade. We must all try to retain the festive spirit in this bleak war.

July 2nd: 50 pure bred White Leghorn pullet chicks are obtained from Thornber Bros. Mytholmroyd, Yorkshire. They came in a box by train and boat to Douglas, to which I am sent to collect them and they finish a 10-hour journey by bus. They are all alive and well when the box is opened. We need them to strengthen our laying flock of 200 hens. Eggs are not rationed in the Isle of Man, but we could sell many more to regular customers in Onchan and Douglas and to callers to the farm.

25
THE WORLD'S BEST JOB

'The zest has gone out of farming. For any farmer to go round his fields today and view his crops brings him no pleasure. The larger and better his fields of wheat, the more useless the whole business appears. Nobody seems to want the food the British farmers are efficiently producing'.

As a teenager I found those words written by farmer-author A. G. Street in his first book, 'Farmer's Glory', and copied them out in my journal of cherished quotations. Street wrote them in 1931, but they could be applicable today. I suppose if I had heeded them in 1936 when I left the Douglas High School I would never have devoted my working life to farming which I still consider despite all its drawbacks to be the best job in the world.

Those of us with no more ambition than to work on a farm for a pittance were regarded as fit for no other career. But I am proud to have been a part of a great industry operated by skilled people who, had they chosen any other profession, would surely have reached the top, such are the dedication and ability required to derive a living from the land and its live-stock.

The 1930s brought a continuing recession in Manx farming, with farms falling derelict because it did not pay to cultivate them. The 1934 Agricultural Marketing Act of Tynwald was a lifeline which res-cued many a farmer from sinking even further, but it is regrettable that it took a world war with all its tragedies to create a demand for food which gave farm folk a real pride in their calling.

In 1949 food was still scarce, and some would be rationed until 1954. Mechanisation was taking some of the hard labour out of farming, but its cost prevented some farmers making full use of it. One farmer, Bob Fargher of Eyreton Farm, Crosby – we become broth-ers-in-law when we married two sisters – was picked by the Manx Government to attend a national confer-ence on the nation's economic development at Ashridge College near Berkhamstead. Agriculture was just one of the industries to be discussed.

On his return Bob wrote in the *Manx Journal of Agriculture*: 'The capital required to finance the farm-ing industry has reached proportions far beyond the means of those directly concerned with the practical side of agriculture.

'The demands on the farm for greater production at ever-rising costs require maximum efficiency from the farmer and his staff.

'The farmer and his workers are demanding the same standard of living as industrial folk but the dete-rioration of farm property during the agricultural depression has never been remedied and now the cost of improvements has reached gigantic figures'.

It was evident from his and other people's remarks that farming was becoming more of a business than a way of life. No longer could a man start farming with a pair of horses, a few basic implements, half a dozen cows, a score of sheep and some old hens which would keep him until he built up their numbers. And those in rural areas would no longer put up with primitive living conditions such as no mains water or electricity supply.

One of the problems of wartime food production was the emphasis on having to grow on farms crops not suited to Manx soils. Wheat, despite A. G. Street's comments of its production in his home county of Wiltshire, was a disaster on all but the best Manx land. On the other hand the Island's lush pastures in summer, allowing some to be conserved for winter feed, suit dairy farming. By 1950 food production was subject to a certain imbalance, and the traditional mixed farm economy was crumbling.

Milk in particular was over-produced, and this led to a problem for the Isle of Man Dairies which by then handled most of the daily supply. Because my uncle was a director of the company I found my work-load increased by the regular turning of cheese stored on one of our lofts.

This diary entry for June 11th 1950 tells the story: 'There is a big surplus of milk on the Island and about 2,000 gallons a day are being manufactured into cheese by the Isle of Man Dairies. The company is deprived of an outlet for liquid milk in England as that country is now self-sufficient and has abolished rationing of milk. All available space at the dairy depot in Spring Gardens, Douglas, is covered by cheese already made and we are helping out by providing storage space. A total of 418 cheeses weighing about 20 tons and worth more than £1,000 at the wholesale price repose on the cow shed loft.

'They have to be turned every other day as part of the ripening process, heavy work because each cheese weighs around one hundredweight. Milk production has been too attractive in recent years and the time has come for a swing back to beef raising especially as meat is still on ration in the shops. The Manx Government has introduced a subsidy on the rearing of beef type calves in an attempt to remedy the problem.'

Meat was scarce and one untapped source was rabbits, that scourge of the Manx countryside, as my diary entry for August 26th 1950, shows: 'One of the greatest nuisances to farmers, the ubiquitous rabbit, is enjoying the limelight of the press and occupying the thoughts of the agricultural community generally.

'Concern is expressed that these pests are multiplying rapidly and doing increasing damage to crops all over the Island. In the war years poaching was a lucrative proposition and this soon reduced the rabbit population.

'Today with frozen Australian rabbits in the shops there is no market for local rabbits and, except for the occasional gunman intent on a day's sport, no one is anxious to hunt.'

Incidentally the word 'gunman', used widely in 1950, is no longer acceptable today because it implies men wielding a weapon in Northern Ireland or some other trouble spot. Now we have to call him a 'shooter.'

The drift from the land was not felt to any great extent in 1950. There were still 1,400 farm workers alongside 1,200 farmers and their families. So it was no great shock when a visiting farmer, Edgar Greenwood from Yorkshire, told Manx farmers at a meeting in Arbory Parish Hall that to grow huge quantities of kale he applied loads of farmyard manure, all forked in by hand. 'The kale stalks are as thick as a man's arm, and we have to cut them with a hedge slasher. To achieve such massive growth we give each plant a hand dressing of sulphate of ammonia. We trickle it directly around each growing plant from a milk bottle.'

Labour was certainly cheap and plentiful when men were available for such attention to an individual plant. In the same year Robert Bruce from Durham assured another farmers' meeting at Crosby that 'the day of surpluses and gluts has gone. The increasing population and the demand for a higher standard of living are going to require every ounce of food. In fact it is our duty to make the maximum contribution.'

History has proved Mr. Bruce, who was county agricultural officer for Durham, wrong but he was not to know the promises the UK Government, was making – when its primary duty was to feed a hungry people – would be broken so quickly once overseas supplies were available.

Some of us heeded Mr. Greenwood's advice that kale was a valuable feed for cows and very high in protein. But cutting it by hand and carting it to the cows was laborious, so we asked why should the animals not do the job for themselves? As with turnips, we found that improved electric fences effectively confined the cattle to a prescribed area and moving the fence daily gave them a fresh untainted 'bite'.

The coming of artificial insemination for cattle led to a proliferation of jokes, the least rude of which are perhaps suitable for retelling here: there was said to be a lady who in all innocence, for instance, told the man from the Board of Agriculture that she had installed a hook in the cowshed where he could hang his trousers...

When the television age dawned, some wag would hang up a message for his cows based on the announcement on TV screens: 'Normal service will be resumed as soon as possible.'

And even before AI reached the Isle of Man in 1943 there was the story of the boy who, arriving at the Dhoon School one morning, was asked by the teacher where he had been the previous day. 'Oh, I had to take a cow to the bull,' he defended himself. 'Couldn't your father have done that?' asked the teacher. 'No,' came the reply, 'It's got to be a bull.'

Although AI reduced the need for keeping bulls on farms, there was still an all-time record entry of 41 bulls at the Spring Show held at the Leighany Field, Ramsey on March 23rd 1950. In those distant days no women ever attended the show, which was confined to male sires such as bulls and stallions. It was considered indelicate for the fair sex to gaze on such animals. On farms, too, women stayed discreetly away from the scene when bulls or stallions were carrying out the duty they were kept for.

So before an all-male crowd the 41 bulls were paraded, of which there were 25 Shorthorns, the pre-

dominant breed on the Island. But there was as yet little interest in the breed which would soon replace the Shorthorn as a milk producer, the British Friesian. There were just two exhibits by pioneers of the breed, Ernest Griffin of Balnahowe, Port Erin, and Harry Comish, Ballastroke, Arbory.

The reason for the record number of bulls was the introduction of a premium of £14 by the Board of Agriculture for every bull which in the opinion of the visiting judge, S.A.C. Eaton from County Tyrone, was of sufficient merit. To qualify the bull had to be paraded at the show and had to be available for use by other farmers. The £14 would help pay for the keep of a bull, which eats twice as much as a cow.

Harry Fozard, Ballaglonney, Braddan, showed the best dairy bull, with Jim Cowin, Middle Farm, Braddan turning out the reserve champion; both were Dairy Shorthorns. Herbie Nelson, Crossacks Farm, Ballasalla, exhibited a Beef Shorthorn to take the beef championship with Harry and Tyson Burrows, White House, Kirk Michael, claiming reserve honours with a Hereford bull.

But if bulls were still numerous, stallions were down to two instead of the dozen shown a few years earlier before the impact of mechanisation. They came from A. E. Crellin, 12 Waterloo Road, Ramsey, showing a Clydesdale, and Douglas vet I. M. Munslow with a Cleveland Bay.

How did I record so much about the day? Well, it was a milestone for me, because as secretary of the Isle of Man Federation of Young Farmers' Clubs I had been invited to speak at the dinner following the show in reply to the toast of Kindred Societies – the first time I had reached such dizzy heights.

Incredible as it may seem in these days of setting land aside from food production, we heard the Governor, Sir Geoffrey Bromet, appeal for the reclamation of more land for agriculture.

'We are very short of food and unless we produce more people in these islands are going to starve,' he warned.

26
A FINE IMPRESSION

It's an ill wind – and out of the great farming depression of the 1930s sprang a youth organisation which attracted thousands of members during the rest of the century. The year 1934 marked the birth of the Island's first two Young Farmers' Clubs in an attempt, alongside the passing of the Agricultural Marketing Act by Tynwald, to restore confidence in a flagging industry.

The Young Farmers' Club idea was not original. The first club in Britain had been started in 1921, and in 1923 young Manxmen were brought together for a cattle-judging competition which the *Daily Dispatch* on August 10th described as 'an outstanding attraction at the Isle of Man Agricultural Society's show in Nunnery Park, Douglas, worthy of copying elsewhere in the country.'

In Ballaugh the district branch of the Royal British Legion encouraged skill in sheep-shearing among farm workers. It promoted an annual sheep-shearing and wool-wrapping competition with all the razzmatazz of a modern sporting event in the form of the Douglas Legion Band. Extra attractions were an ankle competition among the ladies and tug-of-war for the men.

The livestock judging and sheep-shearing competition were well supported, brought together the youth of the countryside, and demonstrated the need for organised clubs.

On the evening of Monday January 8th 1934, when country people were in town for the weekly mart held during the afternoon, Richard Cain, an MHK and staunch supporter of agriculture, addressed a meeting in the United Methodist Hall in Ramsey. He outlined the work of a Young Farmers' Club and urged young people to band together for their own good.

Considerable enthusiasm was shown, and before the evening was over the Northern YFC had been formed with the aim: 'To encourage the agricultural, educational and social advantages of the Northern parish of this Island.' Potential members rushed to pay the annual subscription of 2/6d, although one lad who later became a prosperous farmer and landowner told me he could not pay immediately; he had to give the secretary and treasurer, Edward Kerruish, who was to become a prominent politician, an IOU for his half crown. 'I earned enough in the next few days docking turnips for farmers on piece work to pay it off,' he recalled.

The *Ramsey Courier* welcomed the formation of the club with these words: 'It should be of great value to the younger generation of those interested in agriculture, not only for the social facilities it will provide but also for those events which will be of practical value to all those actively engaged in agriculture.

'It is a hopeful portent for agriculture that the younger members of the industry have had the initiative and the energy to form such an organisation. If the club is successful in developing a closer spirit of

115

co-operation between the members of the agricultural community it will be playing a useful part in laying the foundation for a more prosperous agricultural industry on the Island.'

Elected to office in this pioneering YFC were William C. Christian, a forward-looking farmer and breeder of Shropshire sheep whose fame spread throughout Britain, as president, George Howie, government agricultural organiser, as adviser, Ivor Crowe, Balladoole, Lezayre, chairman, Alfred Corlett, Milan House, Bride, vice-chairman, and Edward Kerruish, Ramsey, secretary and treasurer.

In addition to the officers, the committee comprised Olive Crowe, Lilian Southward, Alfred Christian and Albert Kneen. Members took their horses – no tractors then – to the Sulby Ploughing match on February 1st 1934, and on March 2nd made history with an organised visit to the government's Knockaloe Experimental Farm at Patrick. There they inspected the Shorthorn and Aberdeen Angus bulls imported for sale to farmers, and placed them in order of merit to establish the first Young Farmers' livestock-judging competition.

In May, Northern held the first YFC sheep-shearing with a contest at Vollan Farm, Ramsey, home of founder member Albert Kneen.

Soon young farmers elsewhere wanted their own clubs and in April 1934 Mr. Howie, with two farmers in Marown, Harley Cunningham of Ellerslie, and Joseph Callister, Ballavitchel, spoke at a packed meeting in Crosby Methodist Hall. It was decided to launch the Central YFC, with Stuart Callister as secretary *pro tem*. At a meeting a fortnight later the first officials were installed with Mr. Cunningham as president, Bob Fargher, Ballavargher, Union Mills, chairman, Jack Callister, Ballavitchel, secretary and Charlie Lewin, Ballamillaghyn, Braddan, treasurer.

They were backed by a committee comprising George Kermeen, Kennaa, St. John's, Ben Kelly, Algare, Baldwin, Tom Kinvig, Clybane, The Cooil, Charlie Moore, Ballalough, Baldwin, Cyril McKeown,

Garth Farm, and Leslie Clarke, Rock Farm, both Crosby. Two ladies on the committee were Nora Leedham (later Mrs. Harley Cunningham) and Miss Bastin, a poultry girl at Ellerslie.

In June 1934 the first YFC trip outside the Island took seven members from Northern and three from Central on a farming tour of Scotland organised by Mr. Howie and travel agent W. H. Chapman. At the Royal Highland Show the members watched three Manx girls compete with success in an all-Scotland butter making competition. Ann Quirk from Ballachrink, Dalby, (later Mrs. Jack Moughtin of Peel) was highly commended in her class, while second place prizes went to Betty Teare, the Vaaish Farm, St. John's – later to lead the Manx Women's Land Army during World War Two – and to Florence Corkill, Ballamenagh, Lonan, who married and settled in Scotland.

The two clubs joined for another visit to Knockaloe in July 1934, where the Board of Agriculture was in the second year of its experiments with silage as a winter feed for cattle. 'Silage,' wrote one of the Young Farmers, 'did not arouse much interest but it was believed that it could be a crop which might prove extremely useful in a difficult turnip season.' No one was to know almost 70 years ago that silage would become the most widely used form of fodder, and that turnips would hardly be grown at all.

When the Isle of Man Agricultural Society held its summer show at Milntown, Ramsey, it invited young farmers to compete in judging heavy horses and cattle. The winners were Charles Kerruish of Ballafayle, Maughold, and Bob Fargher, with runners-up Ivor Crowe, Balladoole, Percy Kissack, Ballocowle, Lezayre and Herbert Quark, Ballavoddan, Andreas.

The outbreak of war in 1939 brought a new role for the two YFCs. They were used by the Manx Government for the dissemination of improved farming practice, and for training farmers and their staffs in new skills in the fight to produce more home-grown food. From the ranks of the clubs came the secretaries

116

appointed by government for the 17 parish war agricultural committees.

There was an influx of new YFC material among the 253 girls who joined the Manx Women's Land Army or worked on the land in a private capacity. Young men and women outside the Northern and Central districts often cycled to join in the two clubs' activities; petrol was on ration, and in any case few young people had access to a motor vehicle.

With the onset of another winter and the prospect of long wet rides on rainy nights, another group – encouraged by Central members Annie Kneen from Peel and Henry Quayle from Glenlough Farm, Marown – asked Mr. Howie about the chances of having their own club. He agreed, and 19 youngsters gathered at Baldrine Methodist Hall on December 3rd 1943. Mr. Howie, now in uniform as an officer in the Home Guard and on his way to a parade, addressed the meeting.

The result was the formation of the Lonan & Onchan Young Farmers' Club, subsequently changed to Eastern. John Clague, Ballavarrane, Lonan, was the first chairman, Laurie Kelly, Bibaloe Beg, Onchan (in time to become president of the Manx National Farmers' Union) vice chairman, Jim Quilleash, Ballaragh, Lonan, treasurer and Harvey Briggs, Ballakilmartin, Onchan, secretary.

Other founder members are recorded for posterity as Joe Quine, John Moore, Sidney Kelly, Albert Moore, Arthur Moore, Bob Dobson, Cecil Gorry, John Gorry, John Corlett, Ernest Kelly, Wilfred Callin, Henry Taggart and Bert Corkill with two girls, Joyce Gorry and Jean Quine.

Southern country folk had regarded the Central as their local club, but in 1946 they too decided that they needed their own. An attendance of 52 at the inaugural meeting on February 26th in Arbory Parish Hall confirmed their enthusiasm. The meeting chose Lieut. Col. Clifford Kniveton, MC, as president, Sidney Taggart, Billown Farm, Ballasalla, chairman, John Watterson, Scarlett Farm, Castletown, vice chairman, Doris Gale, Castletown, secretary and Leslie Kinrade, Mull-ny-Quinney, Santon, treasurer.

The fourth club decided on a different form of representation for its committee. Two were to be appointed for the parishes it covered. They were: Arbory – Robert Kinvig and Robert Taggart: Malew – Andrew Kennaugh and Jack Faragher: Rushen – Mona Qualtrough and Robert Kennaugh: Santon – Eddie Christian and Harold Gill.

The clubs have always played a role in Manx life not envisaged by their founders; they became the best dating service ever known. Where better to do a spot of courting than in the back seat of the motor coaches the clubs hired to take members to events? There was no heating in the 'charas', but each pair of seats was provided with a travelling rug in winter by the proprietor, and this was another aid to privacy once the driver turned off the inside lights . . . So YFCs acquired a reputation as a marriage bureau, the efficacy of which I can confirm because I met the girl I would marry at a dance in Castletown organised by the newly formed Southern Club at Christmas 1946.

In addition, the movement encouraged men and women to take their places in rural life outside the confines of the farm. Nervous young speakers would stand for the first time on public platforms, some of them on occasion uttering words they regretted. There was the chairman at a public meeting at Crosby, introducing a visiting vet who was to speak on animal diseases. He began: 'Tonight we are going to have the warble fly, then we're going to have supper, and then we're going to have worms in sheep.'

At least it added a touch of levity to two subjects which, despite their importance to their hearers at the time, were pretty dull and boring in themselves.

But more importantly, this public speaking helped Young Farmers to acquire confidence which in time would prove a huge asset in their careers.

27
WE MADE OUR EXCUSES . . .

As soon as the Isle of Man had four Young Farmers' Clubs, one in each quarter of the Island, there was a need for a central organisation to co-ordinate programmes and to communicate with other people. So in June 1946 George Howie convened a meeting in the Agricultural Marketing Society offices, then just two rooms above the Westminster Bank at the top of Victoria Street in Douglas.

Each club was invited to send four representatives. Those present, with one absentee from Northern, were: Central – Annie Kneen, Henry Quayle, Bob Fargher, Sidney Quirk; Eastern – John Corlett, Ernest Kelly, John Amery, Harvey Briggs; Northern – Sidney Brew, Lance Kneale, Leslie Callow; Southern – Doris Gale, Harold Gill, Robert Kinvig, John Watterson.

It was decided to form the Isle of Man Federation of Young Farmers' Clubs, with each club providing 15/- for its running. They confirmed an upper age limit of 36 for members, but agreed that anyone over that age could be an associate member, entitled to attend meetings but with no voting power.

These rules meant that the government of each club lay in the hands of members themselves, a degree of democracy they appreciated and which, along with their public speaking skills, led to many becoming leaders of the community in later years .

I had cycled into Douglas for the meeting and left my bicycle, unlocked and unguarded, against the wall of the bank. There was no question of anyone stealing it in those days, although we did occasionally have lamps taken until we learned to take them with us.

Bob Fargher from Eyreton Farm, Crosby was elected the first Federation chairman, Annie Kneen from Peel the secretary and I found myself vice-chairman. Transport was difficult, and one of Annie's first jobs was to write to the petrol rationing committee of Tynwald to ask for an allowance so that members could travel to events at their local club. The request was refused and instead they had to pool coupons and share vehicles, frequently squeezing into dilapidated vans stinking of calves, pigs, rotting potatoes and decaying vegetables. On June 1st 1948 the basic petrol ration was increased, much to our delight.

In April 1946 the Young Farmers were invited to submit their views on the future of their industry to a government-appointed commission, one of several set up to prepare a blueprint for agriculture in my lifetime. Like many before and since it spent months weighing up the evidence and came out with a report which could be summed up in one sentence: 'Agriculture must become more efficient.' Amongst hard-working farmers struggling to make a living the advice was not well received.

Following the founding of the Federation, Young Farmers began to spread their wings. Members, some who had never been 'off the sod', very much enjoyed organised tours to study farming first to Nottinghamshire and then a year later to Northern Ireland.

To qualify for a trip, they had to have attended at least 50% of education meetings (dances did not count!), and to qualify for a Board of Agriculture contribution to the cost we had to submit a written report on our return, a stipulation which led to my own interest in writing on farming affairs.

In May 1948 the Manx Federation accepted an invitation to send two delegates to the annual general meeting of the National Federation in London. Bob Fargher and I, as chairman and vice-chairman, were picked and instructed to discuss the question of affiliation which so far had been refused because our upper age limit was 36, while in the UK – apart from Cheshire – it was 26.

Bobby and I each had £12 provided by the Board of Agriculture towards our expenses. It covered most of the cost of the boat to Liverpool, the train to London, and four nights at the Bonnington Hotel in Southampton Row.

It was my first visit to London, but Bobby had been there before. On our first night we sallied forth to see the bright lights of the capital, innocents abroad. We were strolling down a street when we were approached by two well-dressed girls. 'Would you like to enjoy yourselves tonight?' they asked. Bobby looked at me and whispered 'Why not? They probably want company to attend a show or something.'

'Well' said Bobby, 'We don't want to be too late getting back to the hotel. How long will we be?'

On February 11th 1948, 21 Manx farmers flew out of Ronaldsway in three de Havilland Rapide seven-seater bi-planes hired by Arnold Callin of Isle of Man Farmers Limited for a day trip to the Northern Ireland International Ploughing Match at Saintsfield, County Down. By midday, the rain came down in torrents and we all got thoroughly soaked and mud-caked. Prior to taking off from a wartime airfield for the return journey and with night closing in, we had to move cows off the runway. The intrepid adventurers were: left to right standing: Harold Clarke, Billy Moore, a representative of the NI Ploughing Association, Bob Fargher, John Gelling, Herb Cannell, Charlie Lewin, Arnold Callin, John Clelland, Dick Callin, Stanley Gelling, Henry Taggart and John Shimmin. In front: Stephen Crellin, Harvey Briggs, John Clague, Alfred Corlett and Joe Cross.

'As long as it takes!' one girl replied. Bobby and I suddenly realised what kind of enjoyment they were offering, and as they write in the tabloid press, we made our excuses and left . . .

You couldn't really blame our naivety. After all, we had never seen their like on the streets of Onchan or

Representing the Island, Joe Quine took part in an International Ploughing Match in Limavady, Northern Ireland in late 1949.

Crosby. And we could hardly spend Manx government money – the girls wanted £2 each – on such an escapade. On the other hand YFCs are supposed to be educational. Did we miss a chance to learn something new?

Despite these temptations we attended to the serious business of the visit and put our case to the top officials, but they insisted that we had to lower our upper age limit for members to 26 and we had strict orders not to yield on that. It was not until 1981 that a new generation of Young Farmers, led by Gillian Gelling from the Southern YFC, convinced the National Federation that the Isle of Man could affiliate

provided that in national competitions and events it honoured the 26-year age limit. They succeeded where we had failed.

The time had come for Manx Young Farmers to have their own badge, and in 1949 the Federation launched a competition for a suitable design. It was won by Nancy Cowley (later Mrs. Henry Taggart) from Ballacottier, Onchan, who was awarded a £2 prize. The entry from John Lace, Ballawhannell, Bride, was also considered of particular merit and earned him 10/- .

The clubs developed around the national motto 'Good farmers, good countrymen, good citizens', but the Southern went a stage further, quoting Ecclesiastes 1, 'One generation passes away and another generation comes, but the earth stays forever.'

This was the age-old belief that the land remains and there will always be people needed to work it. The continuity of farming was the gospel Young Farmers had to follow, and the Federation in its publications added these words from Dean Swift (1667-1745), 'Whoever would make two ears of corn or two blades of grass to grow upon a spot of ground where only one grew before would deserve better of mankind and do more essential service to his country than the whole race of politicians put together.' To some of us – Keys candidates might do well to heed these views – this implies that politicians are ten a penny, skilled farmers much scarcer.

But few aspiring politicians will worry. The farming vote accounts for just two per cent in total, and a radical change I have witnessed in my lifetime is that no longer can farmers swing an election. By the 1951 election, the YFCs were becoming increasingly involved in politics, to the extent where the Federation adopted a resolution that club platforms should not be used by Keys candidates making election speeches. Apparently some had attended club meetings to speak during their campaigns.

Despite the Isle of Man's continued detachment from UK affairs, Northern area clubs covering eight counties chose Douglas for their annual conference in October 1949. Among the 500 people who attended, giving a useful late boost to the tourist season, was Lord Derby, who had a double interest as president of the movement for England and Wales and as a member of a family who once owned the Island. 'My family thought a lot of the Manx', he told us. 'I hope their influence laid a just basis for those of you now tilling its land.'

We agreed, but only out of politeness, because after all the landlord and tenant situation in 1949 (when 80% of Manx farmers still held their land under harsh leases) was little better than the feudal system inflicted by the Derbys and Stanleys.

So successful was the 1949 conference that it returned to Douglas in 1954, with even greater support. I was still the local secretary, but my allegiance was torn between my unpaid organising duties and our efforts on the farm to save the harvest in the worst weather ever for gathering it. The bulk of our crop was still in the fields at the time of the conference in the second week of October – and would be for many months to come, so persistent was the rain.

The agricultural revolution, which helped to double the amount of food produced on Manx farms and offered the consumer cheap food, brought problems for the YFC movement. Fewer workers on the land were needed as their place was taken by tractors, combine harvesters and milking machines. Of course this lowered the reservoir of potential club members, but visionary new programmes began to attract support from outside the industry.

The Isle of Man suffered employment problems in the 1950s, with many leaving their homeland for work elsewhere. The Governor, Sir Ambrose Dundas, wrote to the Federation in 1953 seeking suggestions to alleviate unemployment, but agriculture had no answer during its own crisis of a new drift from the land.

Charles Kerruish, president of the Manx National Farmers' Union and himself a product of the Northern YFC, invited each of the Island's four clubs to send a delegate to serve on the Union's council. This involvement in political affairs was a huge step forward for a generation brought up in the belief that children – and young people in general – should be seen but not heard. Meanwhile, deep in the countryside itself, the clubs undertook a project for Bristol University. Members plotted the use of every field on the Island for inclusion in a book on the economy written by Dr. J. W. Birch, which is still a standard work of reference.

In 1955 the Federation was awarded a grant from the W.K. Kellogg Foundation of Michigan. The cereal company was prepared to help clubs increase their membership, promote the movement and arrange international exchanges. The grant amounted to £365 per year, a lot of money in those days, and was to continue for five years. It enabled 17 carefully selected members to visit farms in the south west of England and two more, Ken Cringle and Michael Kemp, to travel further afield to Denmark and Sweden where agriculture and food processing were the main industries.

The Kellogg Foundation was impressed by the enthusiasm of Manx Young Farmers, and extended the programme for another year into 1961 when five members, Ian Quayle, Joe Leece, David Clague, Walter Cannell and Harvey Briggs, were sent to collect facts on farming in Scandinavia. We stayed on farms in Denmark and also visited Sweden.

Kelloggs stipulated that some of the money should be used to improve the place of women in farming. Courses were held in cookery, in butter and cheese-making, and in utility poultry, an important enterprise on every farm until a later Manx Government threw the industry to the wolves within the EU.

Mary Radcliffe (now Mrs. Noel Cringle JP) began the Lady Farmers' Group which is still operating. A sign of the passing years is that it began as the Lady Young Farmers' Group but has now dropped 'Young' from its title!

28
BETTER TIMES

I feel privileged to have witnessed the greatest changes ever in life in the Isle of Man, notwithstanding the fact that I am still a 'come-over' in Manx terms; after all, I have only been here since 1926. My wife Laura – indigenous Manx, a Kermode from Laxey – sometimes likes to reminded me of this, asking me do I think I like the Isle of Man, and will I be staying?

Particularly noticeable over recent decades has been the swing in the economy from dependence on the Island's natural resources to the finance sector, with so many people deriving from it a standard of living no one could have envisaged in the past. Full employment is one result of these better times.

It was not always so, as is revealed in a diary entry I made on September 21st 1953. It describes fears about the harvest, tells of booming trade in Ramsey Mart every Monday of the year, but warns of the spectre of unemployment.

September 21st: Torrential rain and gale force south-westerly wind. A day of intermittent downpours of rain with strong winds to drive more water into the already saturated stooks of corn. The oats are deteriorating fast and will soon be unsaleable. Most of the farming community are glad of an excuse to get away from it all, judging by the large crowd at Ramsey Mart. Not away from the rain because there is plenty of that in Ramsey, but away from the sight of crops being ruined in the fields. Trade is good in the mart, with brisk bidding for store, cattle and breeding sheep. There are not enough of either for buyers. Despite these mixed prospects in farming, let us be thankful that we are not confronted with a winter of idleness and shortage of money like the 1,000 unemployed in the Isle of Man today.'

Although most of my diary is confined to affairs connected with the farm, I sometimes record happenings further afield. On February 2nd 1953, I wrote that the weekend had been a black one for Britain. A great gale had brought death and destruction. It struck the motor vessel *Princess Victoria* on passage from Stranraer to Larne, causing her to founder with the loss of 128 lives, although 44 survivors were plucked by rescuers from the turbulent Irish Sea. On the east coast of Britain abnormally high tides drowned 250 people and flooded 250,000 acres of farmland.

Sweet rationing ended on February 12th after being in force for 10 years, except for a period of three months in 1949 when it was relaxed, only to be re-imposed because not enough sweets and chocolate could be made to meet the demand.

On June 2nd we had the Queen's coronation. After watching the procession to Westminster Abbey at the Regal Cinema in Victoria Street, Douglas (television in those days was still confined to London and the Home Counties) I declared: 'A royal procession genuinely cheered in this way is better than a dictator's show of armed strength.'

On the farm we decided to invest in a more modern tractor and it was delivered on March 11th, as I recorded: 'Our first tractor, FMN 522, one of the old type of Fordson, was bought in 1943. From then it has done most of the arable work with very little mechanical attention. Last April it was fitted with a reconditioned engine. We are keeping this Fordson, bought new on steel wheels for £190, but sold in part exchange another Fordson, EMN 227, which we purchased second hand in Ramsey Mart last December.

'Our new tractor from Quayle's Garage, Hill Street, Douglas, is a Nuffield Model M4 fitted with rubber tyres, hydraulic lift, power take-off, lights and self starter, all huge improvements in tractor design. It runs on vapourising oil, a form of paraffin. It is being forecast that all future tractors will run on diesel fuel and that they will supersede vapourising oil engines. But a VO Nuffield costs £595 and a diesel £150 more - a big increase in capital expenditure which the diesel supporters say will be soon recovered by lower fuel consumption and the use of cheaper fuel.'

So we had a powerful new tractor for the heavy spring work, and the horses spent more time at grass. We were reluctant to sell them and, except as horse meat in a hungry Britain, they would not command much of a price. In time our three faithful friends ended their days peacefully in old age but the younger ones no longer needed were sold.

It was at pulling the binder, hard work for three horses walking abreast, that the extra power was needed, but there was one snag. The horses would stop of their own accord when they felt any obstruction in the workings of the machine which cut the corn and delivered it in sheaves. But the tractor stormed on, sometimes causing expensive breakages.

On May 12th, when our half-yearly rent was due, my diary shows some sympathy for landowners although as tenant farmers we were in their grasp: 'Landlords, it is said, are poor men these days; the tenant is said to have the best end of the stick. Certainly there has been little increase in farm rentals over the past 30 years, and landlords have only joined in the

increased prosperity of agriculture when they have chosen to sell property.'

Four days later I was lamenting the poor support for the Manx National Farmers' Union, the political arm of agriculture founded in 1946: 'I hear that the annual general meeting of the Union attracted only 26 loyal members, about 2.5 % of the total number of farmers on the Island. Obviously the other 97.5 % considered the meeting had little to offer. Some, like me, are members but confine active participation to the occasional branch meeting.

'It is however only too true, as our critics tell us, that Manx farmers cannot or will not work together for the ultimate benefit of the industry. Farming is not in such a prosperous condition that we can afford to neglect this opportunity of uniting once and for all. Petty jealousies and cussedness can only result in us continuing to be the laughing stock of the community'.

Yet the union was campaigning to protect the interests of farmers, and one of its problems was trying to balance the output of Manx food to supply a local population and the thousands of 'visitors' from June to September. Farmers produced for that market until 1939 when the outbreak of war changed demand to all the year round, and many more mouths to feed, with an influx of service people and enemy aliens.

Pigs are the easiest species to multiply quickly, with each sow capable of breeding 20 or more piglets a year. In 1953 there were more than were needed for pork and export markets were sought. The pigs came from mixed farms with two or three sows and from a new feature of Manx farming, specialised breeding units. In an adventurous move Jack Woods of W.H. Woods & Son set up a bacon factory with a weekly intake of 100 pigs. In the same year the Isle of Man Pig Producers Association was formed, a modern version of which still operates.

Potatoes, eggs and oats were all in over-supply, and in an attempt to find a market in the UK, union president Charles Kerruish met the Governor, who agreed to approach the Home Office in London to ask for special terms for Manx produce. The reply was that it would be bought only at the same price as that paid for supplies from other foreign countries. This led to further calls for 'English prices and conditions', with the Manx Government making up the difference and virtually paying the cost of export, which it refused to do.

Yet cattle were scarce, both for milk and beef. The cheese ration still stood at 1¹/₅ ounces per person per week, with a retail price of 1/4d per pound. Beef, although no longer rationed, was so scarce that in August 1953 600 live cattle were imported from Ireland to feed the tourists; there was, of course, an outcry from local farmers who accused Government Office, which had issued import permits, of gross mismanagement. There were enough cattle on Manx farms, said the union, but they alleged that butchers wanted the cheaper Irish beef without the hassle of running around the Island looking for Manx.

The union discussed the situation and laid the foundation of a fatstock scheme devised by Deemster Ramsey Johnson. It was eventually launched in 1955 and operates to this day.

'Manx agriculture is at the crossroads,' declared Charles Kerruish. He told the council of the union that the Governor was keen to develop cooperative marketing. The union decided to organise visits to cooperative ventures in the UK and in June 1953 a party of 30 farmers, mainly from the union but with representatives of the Agricultural Marketing Society, the Pig Producers Association and the Farmers' Club, toured Staffordshire, Warwickshire, Shropshire and Herefordshire to see successful systems.

The union agreed to a request from the Agricultural Wages Board for an increase of 3d. per hour for farm workers to bring their weekly wage up to £6.8s.4d. from £5.14s.4d. The wage still compared badly with that of other workers, particularly those in government jobs, but most men preferred farming to joining the ranks of the growing unemployed.

The shortage of work brought a lad of 20 to knock on our farmhouse door looking for a job just before Christmas 1953. I wrote: 'My uncle gave him a job docking turnips at 1/- per 100 yards of ridge. He lives in Douglas and travels by bus each day bringing his own food but my aunt gives him "lunch" mid-morning and mid-afternoon of a jug of tea, jam sandwiches and a slice of pastry or cake.'

On December 29th I wrote that he had worked over the Christmas holiday and docked enough turnips to feed the cattle for a month. We had no more work for him, and as he picked up his wages he was almost in tears. But at least he had enough for the boat fare – steerage – to Liverpool, where he intended to look for a job.

THE WHITE BRIDGE

A new development in 2001 was an underpass to the White Bridge connecting Groudle and Molly Quirk's glens. In 1953 you walked the river at your peril, as this diary entry of May 17th suggests: 'Not many yards from Ballakilmartin is the White Bridge, a landmark for travellers on the Ramsey-to-Douglas road. Few motorists know that in the river it traverses, the boys of Onchan spent many happy hours tickling trout. The first bridge on the site was built by a vicar of Onchan about 1635. According to the church wardens in a report to Bishop Foster he had not lived with his wife for 11 years and was accused of fathering the child of a village girl.

'To cleanse his guilt and ensure his entry into heaven he agreed to build a bridge across the river at a point most convenient for the parishioners. It was to be coloured white as a mark of penance. The first bridge was made of wood and was, the wardens said, "as good a deede as ever was done in these parts".

'The White Bridge Hill was notorious for highway robbers in the past. My wife's great-grandmother, returning to their farm at Agneash from Douglas market on a dark winter's night with her husband, was thrown out of her trap when robbers tried to stop the horse. Her hip was broken and the money obtained for the week's produce stolen'.

125

Fred Cooil's Marshall engine and Marshall mill threshing at Ballrhenny, Port Erin in 1907. (Photo: Stephen Carter)

Mill days were a part of the Manx agricultural heritage for over a century. They began when the first travelling mills and an engine to drive their mechanism were pulld from farm to farm by horses.

By the 1880s, the engines were improved and were able to move under their own power and tow the threshing mill and, in time, a straw baler, too. The mills visited each farm in turn and neighbours from other farms provided the fifteen or so men needed to operate a mill. When the outfit visited another farm the 'help' would be returned.

Each mill stay was a social occasion in the district and although hard work, was welcomed as a break from the tedium of winter on the farm. Only the womenfolk detested them - they had to provide midday dinner and tea as well as morning and afternoon 'lunches' for a crew of hungry men.

Mill days gradually disappeared with the arrival of the combine harvesters which can cut and thresh in one operation. They arrived on the Isle of Man in 1944 when John Clelland of Lanjaghen, Onchan and brothers harry and Tyson Burrows at White House Farm, Kirk Michael bought Massey Harris machines. But it took another 40 years for the combines to completely replace the traditional sheaf and stook method of harvesting.

29
A RACE DAY WINNER

Kelly's Noted Herb Beer was the chief thirst-quencher in my youth. Non-alcoholic, it was brewed by Bill Kelly to a secret recipe in a shed in the quarry opposite his home in the front street of Cronkbourne Village. He sold it from his house, or in high summer from a table outside the door, together with home-made lemonade and a full range of patent medicines for every ill.

Mrs Kelly, as portly as her husband, had been born and reared at Mount Rule, a couple of miles inland from Cronkbourne but still in the parish of Braddan. She must have been a girl around 1860, and she used to tell me that in spring the Baldwin shepherds would come down from the hills when the pressure was off after the lambing season and before shearing began. 'They wouldn't have seen a face of clay all winter and no woman was safe from them,' she said.

It was a story I often tell to today's Baldwin shepherds, Philip Caley and Graham Crowe, despite the fact that I believe them to be respectable family men – as confirmed by one being appointed Captain of the Parish of Braddan, and the other serving as President of the Manx National Farmers' Union from 1989-94.

When I attended the Douglas High School at St. Ninian's, from 1931-1936, we had just one day off in TT week, for Friday's senior race. But on the other two race days the school was well placed for keen young fans, and we rarely concentrated on much class work during Monday's junior and Wednesday's light-weight. On the race days we were at school I took my dinner in with me, because I could not cross the closed roads and cycle home; I always used to carry a bottle of Kelly's Noted Herb Beer to drink with my sandwiches.

Now Mr. Kelly often used real beer bottles, sealing them with a cork when his own supply was exhausted, and on one occasion mine happened to carry the name of Heron & Brearley. I remember I was sitting with other boys alongside the railings in the school playing-field, watching the races and eating my dinner, when an officious prefect spotted my bottle.

Believing it to contain real beer (the colour was similar) he rushed off to tell my form master, who hurried out of the school building to see for himself. Try as I might, I failed to convince him that it was not real beer and was not alcoholic. He ordered me to accompany him to the headmaster's study. There he told of finding this boy drinking beer to Arthur (always known as Bill after the Dickens character) Sykes, who listened patiently before dismissing the master. I then repeated my explanation.

'Kelly's Noted Herb Beer?' he asked. 'Yes, I know it well.' Mr. Sykes lived at a house called Glion Beg at the foot of Bray Hill and was a frequent walker to Cronkbourne and Tromode, about a mile away. I had even seen him partaking of refreshments at Bill Kelly's house himself.

'Look here, Briggs', he said. 'Next time bring

Downward's Lemonade or Dandelion & Burdock like the other boys. We don't want the school gaining a reputation for under-age drinking, do we? Oh, and I'll keep the bottle.'

And he did, probably enjoying the contents and retaining the bottle for return to Bill Kelly so that he could claim one penny on his next walk to Cronkbourne! I had an idea he was scoffing at both the sleechiness of the prefect and the pomposity of the teacher.

We drank a lot of herb beer at Ballabeg Farm, because Bill Kelly collected herbs from our fields and most mornings in summer we delivered potatoes by horse and cart to his premises for his 'spud round.' Even when the price of potatoes was fixed in 1934 by the new Agricultural Marketing Act of Tynwald, undercutting was rife among farmers – they were desperate to sell them on an overloaded market – and I fancy the herb beer was part of the deal at settling-up time with my uncle for potatoes bought.

The beer, which would not pass today's hygiene standards but to the best of my knowledge never killed anyone, was particularly welcome at harvest time. There was a lot of hard work in those golden harvests of the past – golden because that was the stage of colour the grain was cut at, first with a scythe around each field to make a 'road' for the binder and the three horses which pulled it.

The binder delivered neat sheaves onto the ground, from which we picked them up and set them in rows of symmetrical stooks, each stook consisting of eight or 10 sheaves depending on where you lived. Eight was sacrosanct on farms in the centre of the Island, 10 more common in the north and south where crops were generally heavier and sheaves more numerous.

In 1953 I estimated that there were 20 combine harvesters at work on Manx farms, but we were still with the majority of farmers in using the traditional sheaf-and-stook method to gather our 30 acres of oats, then still the most widely grown cereal in the Isle of Man.

Here is one of my last reports on a conventional harvest before combines became predominant:

August 20th: Here we are ready to start the corn harvest, although we still have eight loads of hay in rucks in the field. We shall need to get them home first.

August 24th: Cutting roads around oats in track field with scythe to clear a passage for the binder.

August 25th: Today's start in the harvest with our Albion binder and new Nuffield tractor is not a happy one. The mechanism which enables the forks to throw out the sheaf on the binder has developed trouble since it was last working a year ago. The Albion agent, Clague & Craine in Douglas, has not a spare part in stock but arranges for one to be flown over from Leigh in Lancashire within a few days. Meanwhile the Douglas blacksmith, Humphrey ('Andy') Joughin repairs the worn part.

August 26th: Mr. Joughin turns up at the farm to fit the repaired part. Everything appears to be going well and four acres are cut before it breaks again.

August 28th: Frustration indeed. The part flown over for the binder turns out to be the wrong one.

August 30th: 'Six days shalt thou labour' say the scriptures, but here we are working on a Sunday to make up for time lost by the temperamental binder. The forks are operating well, but now the knotter is giving trouble and we have as many loose sheaves as are tied. So back to making bands of straw to bind each sheaf by hand. Serves you right for working on the Sabbath, says an unhelpful neighbour.

August 31st: 1.65 inches of rain fell today according to the Douglas meteorological department, to make it one of the wettest days on record.

September 1st: Fitting new knotter to Albion binder. It cost £10, the equivalent of seven sacks of oats.

September 3rd: Finished cutting corn in Big Gib. In changing the binder from cutting to carriage position we disturb the big wheel, and it is only after a couple of hours' manipulation that we return it to its correct setting.

September 4th: A cloudy day with no noticeable wind and the atmosphere is still and clear as only September and October can provide. It is not dry enough to cut the 'Onward' oats in the Big Garey and the crop is now flattened by heavy rain. As a result many of the heads have been beaten off and now lie in the ground.

September 5th: Another wetting of the long-suffering grain, but even those using combine harvesters are in trouble too. Jack Clelland who bought one of the first two combines in 1944 tells me that for the first season since they started to use it most of the grain will need drying artificially. In other years by selecting suitable days they have always ensured that the oats would be dry enough to store, but there has not been such weather this year.

September 9th: All corn now cut and stooked. The spirit of co-operation among farmers is always more noticeable in practical farming than in politics and marketing. When we heard that our neighbour, Eddie Cooke at Bibaloe Moar, required an extra tractor we offered him the use of our Fordson, not needed in our harvest. Mr. Coole brought the fourth combine harvester to the Island in 1948 and has a large International tractor for pulling it and a Cletrac crawler for hauling the pick-up baler. With both tied up he needed another tractor for the straw turner and collected our Fordson yesterday. Another International tractor he borrowed from Philip Quayle plunged over a bank into Groudle Glen when it was left unattended. We helped to haul it back up a steep slope using Ernest Kelly's Field Marshal tractor equipped with a winch and wire rope, but it is extremely unlikely it will work again.

September 10th: A grand harvest day. The countryside is alive with action. All our neighbours are busy 'carting in.' With all the setbacks this year, corn cutting is less laborious than before the invention of the self binder. When corn was cut by sickle or scythe the cut-ting and binding of sheaves by hand was the hardest part of the harvest and the completion of this was celebrated as the Mhelliah. Today we reckon the Mhelliah is when the last sheaf is in the stack. An ideal harvest team comprised three scythemen, three gatherers or 'lifters' of the cut corn, two tying the sheaves with bands of corn, one stooker and one raker. Women would be as numerous as men, and the youngest girl on the field was presented with a corn dolly made out of the last scythe swathe.

September 14th: Harvest progress at last. Three friends, Fletcher Craine from Douglas, Charlie Looney and Tom Corteen from Maughold, give up some of their holidays from their regular jobs to bring our harvest staff up to five. Our three helpers will be available tomorrow but a bad weather forecast on BBC radio and a falling barometer are ill omens. 10pm: The rain has already arrived.

September 20th: No worthwhile harvest progress for a week. We still have three quarters of our crop in stooks in the field. The overall picture is that 50% of the grain crop is still at risk. Of the 17,500 acres of cereals grown, 14,000 are of oats.

September 26th: Both yesterday and today we made fruitless excursions to the corn fields with tractor and trailer. The sheaves of oats were shaken out to catch what little sun and wind the day brought, but by mid-afternoon they were no dryer. So back to moving stooks to fresh ground to prevent damage to both the sheaves and the young grass with which some of the fields are undersown.

September 27th: Following the increase in the number of combine harvesters on the Island to around 20 there is a glut of oats on the market at the one time. With no government price control in the Isle of Man following the UK's decision to decontrol its grain trade, merchants are offering only 14/- per hundredweight. The UK authorities introduced a new deficiency payment which guarantees farmers 24/- for oats, a huge improvement on our prices. A lot of Manx oats is shipped to Liverpool, where according to the *Liverpool Daily Post* trade in oats is stagnant. We who harvest by sheaf and stook will be able to keep oats in the stack until prices improve. Without adequate storage space for grain on farms, combine users must sell. No wonder most farmers still stick to the old ways despite the ease of harvesting with a combine.

September 30th: Our parish church harvest festival will be held next Sunday. In fairness to the vicar of Onchan, the Reverend John Duffield consulted us about the date as recently as last Saturday. Although there is little hope of harvest being completed before the planned date, we take the view that this is a thanksgiving for all our blessings, and not specifically the corn harvest. Those who talk of the festival being a mockery in view of the corn in the fields are adopting a parochial attitude not consistent with the Christian spirit.

After more frustrating days shaking out sheaves to get them dry enough to stack I eventually reported on October 10th that all was safely gathered in, adding: 'Perhaps my harvest saga has not been in the best traditions of either good literature or sensational journalism, but maybe it will be of interest to readers in years to come when mechanisation has finally taken the hard work and risk out of harvesting.

'Believe me that day will come when we all own combines and there are sufficient drying plants to make grain storage safe.'

Prophetic indeed! But what I did not foresee was that 1953 was just the curtain-raiser for the worst harvest of the century, a fact I can confirm at the dawn of a new one. It had such a profound effect on Manx agriculture that it deserves a chapter in history of its own.

30
ON THE BRINK OF RUIN

'Perhaps when we are very old we will tell people about the year when half the corn in the Isle of Man was still in the fields on Hollantide Day.' That's what I wrote in my journal on November 12th 1954. The harvest of 2000 came close to the disaster of 1954, but by then we were in a new century and harvesting methods had changed so much that it is hard to make a valid comparison.

So, based on memories handed down to me when I was a young man, followed by my own records of every year since 1939, I can state without fear of contradiction that 1954 was the worst harvest of the 20th century. Many farmers were driven to the edge of bankruptcy and some toppled over the brink. Others survived, but lost heavily both in terms of money and their faith in the future of farming.

It was all due to the relentless rain which began in early September and continued with few breaks until Christmas. Fifty years ago Manx farming relied heavily on crops of oats used for livestock feeding and for cash sales. About 13,500 acres were grown annually among a total cereal acreage of 15,000. The demand came from owners of the many horses working on farms and in the towns, and from contracts to porridge makers such as Quaker Oats.

The Isle of Man and Scotland were climatically suited to the production of oats and their farmers were the best at growing the crop. Frequent shipments left the Island's ports for the UK. The trade earned money for farmers, the agricultural merchants, the shipping companies and the general economy of the Island.

At the time it could not be predicted that the acreage of oats would diminish to today's 900 acres, or that it would be replaced by barley and wheat as the market changed.

Believe it or not, in the 1950s none of us ever thought that working horses on the farms or on the roads would ever be completely ousted by machines. Nor did we expect porridge to give way to other cereals at breakfast. 'Get this porridge under your ribs and you'll be able to face the day.' But the age-old advice from mother, who had risen early to make it, was to be replaced by 'Help yourself to cornflakes. I'm too busy to cook anything!'

Now the year 1954 should go down in history for more than a disastrous harvest. The Board of Agriculture was anxious to persuade farmers to grow potatoes which could be sold to other farmers as seed for a new crop in the following year, and it brought Dr. A. Brunton from Scotland to tell them how they could earn an extra £4 per ton by selling certified seed instead of unloading ware (eating) potatoes onto a saturated market.

As with oats, the Isle of Man and Scotland had an advantage over England in the production of seed potatoes, because of the absence in the north of Britain of the aphids which attacked crops elsewhere. A thriving export trade in seed potatoes was developed until it was lost when scientists developed ways of killing the aphids with chemicals and the Island lost its natural advantage.

Poultry keepers, and they included practically every farmer in the Island, were in trouble, as I wrote on January 24th: 'There is a crisis for egg producers. Eggs are plentiful due to the mild winter and the introduction of the battery and deep litter systems which encourage hens to lay whatever the weather outside the shed. Until now a wholesale distribution firm, W.H. Woods & Son, has been buying eggs from farms and preserving them by cold storage for future use. Now the storage is full. Exportation is out of the question because of price differences between Manx and English eggs. Retail price on the Island is 5/6d per dozen, in England it is 3/6d. This is not due to any greater efficiency in production. It is down to a UK Government subsidy totalling £1,250,000 a year, something we have never had in the Isle of Man.'

Another crop suggested, but not grown in the Island until John Bregazzi and pioneer farmers developed it 30 years later, was the growing of bulbs for transplanting in houses and gardens. A visiting speaker, P.G. Meuwissen, assistant agricultural attache at the Dutch Embassy in London, on a tour organised by the Board of Agriculture, described how Holland relied on exports of cheese, butter, tinned milk and cream, bacon, eggs and flower bulbs. He could see no reason why the Isle of Man could not produce bulbs for an unsatisfied market in the UK.

The soil was ideal, he said, except for hyacinths which needed the sandy loams we did not possess. But a suggestion from a group of Young Farmers – no doubt with visions of pretty Dutch girls in native costumes – that the Manx Government should send a party to Holland to see farming for themselves did not receive favour.

The mill moved into the district around Onchan village in January and stayed a fortnight threshing on adjacent farms. We hurried across the fields to be with them for an 8am start, and stumbled home in the dark around 7pm after tea, shouldering our own pitchfork which we never left for anyone else to use.

A young boy was a newcomer one mill day. Boys and girls could leave school at 14 years of age in those days, and most did, because their families needed the money they could earn. 'You should go to the social at Baldrine tonight,' some of the lads suggested. The boy agreed, but did not turn up. Next morning, still threshing at the same farm, he was asked why.

'Oh' he replied, 'the cat defecated in my shoe.' Except that the word he used was not defecated. 'The stink was awful.' Like all of us, he had only one pair of decent shoes. It was some weeks before he resumed his limited social life.

The womenfolk liked threshing on a Saturday because by custom the mill crew of about 15 needed only a 'tea dinner' of plates of cold meat, perhaps some homegrown beetroot, HP sauce and piles of bread and butter – it was always butter, never margarine, in loyal support of a farmer somewhere in the world.

Nor did they need to cook rice or boiled puddings for a Saturday, as they did for the hot dinners of the rest of the week. The men complained when there were no hot dinners, but there was some consolation in that the mill stopped work at 4pm on a Saturday instead of 6pm on other days, enabling them to go home and change ready for a night in town – Douglas in our case – and the pictures.

The threshing needed to be completed before the busy spring work began. On March 12th I wrote, 'A few days of spring-like weather, and activity increases on the land. There is a lot of work to be done and little time to lose if the crops are to go into the ground at the right time.

'Much as we deplore the passing of the picturesque horse from the farming scene we give thanks for the power of tractors. For when land work is pressing the tractor never tires like a horse, nor does the man who drives it experience the same degree of fatigue. Still there is plenty of manual work – trimming hedges, docking turnips, loading manure and feeding cattle. True, there are machines to do these jobs, but to invest in them is to tie up capital better used for the purchase of other things, particularly livestock which grow into money.'

The Isle of Man's envied animal health encouraged farmers to breed animals for export, and before emphasis settled on cattle and sheep, pigs had a brief hour of glory. One incoming farmer, Mike Godfrey, identified a market for the Landrace breed and stayed to make a huge contribution to Manx agriculture. Here is the first we heard about him, as recorded in my journal for March 16th 1954: 'Fashions in livestock breeding are almost as changeable as those in ladies' clothes. At the moment everyone is clamouring for Swedish or Danish Landrace pigs.

'The British Government, prompted by the National Pig Breeders Association, is anxious to protect the interest of British pig breeds and are restricting importations from other countries. The only batch allowed into Britain recently realised fantastic prices at auction, breeding pens of three sows and a boar reaching £2,000. A few sows and gilts bred from previous importations are selling at £300 per head. But no restrictions on importation to the Isle of Man apply, and we are now being regarded as a back door through which Landrace can enter Britain.

'The only restriction on bringing Landrace into the Isle of Man is that the planes bringing them should not touch down anywhere else in the UK. So the Island must have an opportunity to establish itself as a stud farm breeding top class pigs. Messrs. Cussons, who farm Ellerslie at Crosby, are making the most of this and are flying in 20 Swedish Landrace this week. They have been bought by Michael Godfrey, farm manager, for about £100 per head.'

Soon the harvest was upon us although it started later than usual, as my diary tells:

August 30th: Cutting roads around oats in meadow with scythe and making sheaves by hand to make way for the tractor and binder.

September 1st: All our oats is still too green to cut with the binder.

September 3rd: This is the latest start to harvest since I began writing a diary in 1939. Except in 1942 and 1962 we have always been cutting by mid-August.

September 9th: No harvest progress due to rain but this gives me a chance to watch the Manx Grand Prix. George Costain rides to victory in the senior. The driving rain and wet roads are a severe test for man and machine. Another local man, Derek Ennett, wins the junior.

September 21st: Began cutting corn with Albion binder pulled by Nuffield tractor.

September 27th: First two loads of oats carted for stacking in the haggart.

September 28th: Shaking out sheaves to dry but a heavy shower of rain at 6pm soaks them and brings all our work to naught.

October 10th: National Federation of Young Farmers' Club's Northern area conference in Douglas. Fortunately most of our arrangements go according to plan, but my regret is that as secretary of the Manx Federation I am unable to attend some of the events due to harvest preoccupations.

October 22nd: Since we finished cutting our 30 acres of corn on September 27th we have managed to cart home very little and have saved only two small stacks so far. Very few days pass without some rain, and no sooner do we make use of a little drying wind than down comes the rain. Only now and again does the weather go berserk like this, thank goodness.

November 4th: Twenty acres of sodden sheaves much of it with green sprouts lie rotting in the fields. But let us count our blessings. We have a lot of good hay, a fair crop of turnips plus rape and rye-grass for winter keep.

November 8th: Rain, continuous and heavy. 'While the earth remaineth seed time and harvest and cold and heat and summer and winter and day and night shall not cease' – Genesis. No comment at this stage.

November 16th: We are now carting sodden sheaves to the cattle in the sheds for them to browse over, but they eat little of the blackened and mouldy material and we have to dump much in the midden.

November 18th: We patiently plod on with this disastrous harvest, keeping to the pattern we have adhered to since September, namely shaking out sheaves to catch what little drying there is, picking out a few now and again as fit for the stack and re-stooking the remainder to keep the heads off the ground.

November 27th: Rain and storm from 2pm ruins the rest of the corn. Severe gale in evening strips the thatch off the two stacks we had saved. There is no winning this year.

December 1st: Every year since 1939 I have marked the end of our corn harvest by writing in large letters in my diary 'Harvest home'. Then the last sheaf was safely in the stack and a glow of elation settled over the farm. The last date this ever appeared was October 15th in 1942. Then came 1954 and no true end to harvest and little to celebrate. I cannot feel justified in calling this the end of harvest because much of the crop remains in the field, but we can gather no more. What remains will have to be ploughed in, although that in itself will be difficult. But unless we clear the fields we will lose next year's crops, too. We are not alone. Throughout the north of England a disastrous corn harvest drags on, and many farmers lost their hay too.

31
UNFORGETTABLE TIMES

A total of 281 women, not counting farmers' wives, worked on Manx farms during the 1939-45 war, many of them in the government-organised Manx Women's Land Army. In 1985 my wife Laura wrote the following description of her experiences as a Land Girl to mark the 40th anniversary of the ending of the war in Europe:

It was the last day of the 1941 school year. In the assembly hall I moved along the line of girls shaking hands for the last time with Miss Hasler, our headmistress.

After six years at the High School for Girls, tears prickled at the back of my eyes, and a lump rose in my throat as I realised I was leaving my schooldays behind. What made it worse was the feeling that I had let my teachers down, as well as the disapproval I had met with when a few weeks earlier, at the age of 16, I had told my parents that I wanted their permission to enlist in the Manx Women's Land Army.

They were expecting greater things of me, no doubt, and only one of my teachers expressed the wish to be doing what I was going to be involved in.

One day earlier in the term I had had an interview in Victory House for a position in an insurance firm. I came out of the building after taking the application tests and met George Howie, the then agricultural organiser, who at the time was trying to establish a supply of female farm workers to replace the men who by now had volunteered or been conscripted for

the forces. Knowing my love of farming and of animals he suggested I join his newly formed WLA.

And so on September 3rd 1941, as recruit No 5, I presented myself at 7am at Knockaloe Experimental Farm to start six weeks of training which would prepare me for what lay ahead.

All trainees were to receive 30/- per week (£1.50) but as the digs at Patrick cost 25/- (£1.25), I was left with only 5/- (25p) for the bus fares home, clothes, etc.

At the beginning of my training, which really amounted to general farm work, there were two other girls at Knockaloe: Annie Kneen who was in charge of the considerable poultry enterprise, and Erica Christian (later Mrs. Robert Curphey) who became leader of the WLA. Annie it was who taught me to wring a fowl's neck, pluck it, draw it (remove its innards), dress it and present it in its naked glory ready for the oven.

Poultry day was regarded as the great 'itch day'! Fowls always have fleas and lice on them, and in the plucking process they transfer to the handler. Although not living long on their human hosts, they can cause great discomfort while they run around.

As Knockaloe had only a limited number of milking cows, it was arranged that the trainees should receive their hand-milking tuition at Pete Kelly's farm, Shenvalley on the other side of the Patrick Road.

Poor long-suffering cows – to have to put up with the indignity of absolute raw recruits, sitting on a stool

Staff in the poultry unit at Knockaloe Experimental Farm in 1940 prior to the founding of the Manx Women's Land Army. Annie Kneen, secretary of the Central Young Farmers' Club for 13 years is wheeling the barrow, Margaret Kneale (later Mrs Sable) is on the left of the picture and Erica Christian (now Mrs Curphey) eventually leader of the Manx WLA completes the hard-working trio.

with a bucket between their knees, trying in vain to extract a stream of sweet-smelling, steamy milk. I had been lucky enough to learn the art earlier at my brother-in-law's farm at Lonan, so it was a pleasure at the afternoon's milking to fill the buckets.

When the cows were milked we were given 'lunch' in the farmhouse, of fresh, crusty bread and butter, with home-made jam and cake to follow. The late afternoon sun poured through the big kitchen window and reflected back off the lustre jugs and delph on the old dressers. Those were happy days.

One thing we were warned about. It was forbidden

to speak to, or take any notice of, the 18B internees who came out from Peel under armed escort to work at Shenvalley. When I was there they were lifting the potato crop. Some of them looked bedraggled, some sad and some defiant, but in the main they evoked more pity than scorn. One night later on, after being at the pictures in Peel, I was glad to put distance between myself and the camp in which they were housed, when they rioted. The sub-human clamour removed from that mob all pity that I had felt for them in their imprisonment.

The six weeks I spent at Knockaloe passed quickly. One of the most unusual jobs we did was the threshing of some hay to gather cocksfoot seeds for replanting. Sometimes I would go round the sheep with the farm steward, Mr. Bobby Gale. He took great pride in the flock and it was a pleasure to walk the upper fields of the farm to check their numbers and condition.

A new piggery was about to be built, so I spent a few days with him digging out the foundations. Looking back now, I realise that our training was to attune our muscles to the rigorous work we would be expected to do and to break us in gradually to unaccustomed conditions.

My training came to an end when one day Mr. Howie drove me down to Ballamona Moar, Ballaugh, where I was to work. On the way I was dying to ask questions about the place but as he was a quiet, shy man and I was a quiet, shy, immature teenager very few words were exchanged. He left me there to get acquainted with Mr. and Mrs. E.C. Kneen, my future employers. After an hour or two I returned to St. John's by train and walked the rest of the way to Patrick.

The following day, Friday, I was allowed home to spend a long weekend with my family before starting my wartime work in earnest. When the bus conductor dropped me off on the doorstep and handed out my suitcase, my parents thought that I had been released because I hadn't made the grade.

At the beginning of the next week I left Lonan and travelled to Ballaugh by bus via Ramsey, Sandygate and the Cronk. That afternoon I met Louie Corkill, the horseman, for the first time, the only other worker on the farm beside Mr. Kneen.

Next morning I was awakened at 5.45am to help with the hand-milking of the 16 shorthorn cows. It was not such a burden as it might seem, for I loved getting my head against the warm flank of a cow and gradually filling the pail with twin jets of frothy milk. After the milking the bucket-fed calves slurped their way through their milk ration and the racks in their pens were filled with sweet-smelling hay.

The cows were fed with whole or sliced turnips, rolled cereals and cattle cake, and hay for afters. That chore completed, the cowsheds were mucked out, the cows bedded down and the beef cattle in the loose boxes watered, fed and bedded with straw. The pigs, too, received their rations and when all the stock had been tended we then went for our breakfast at around 8.15am.

Louie would attend to the stable, cleaning out, feeding and watering the horses. If there was field work to be done he would harness up directly after his meal and would start straight away on that day's particular job.

During the winter and spring months the yard work was much heavier than in the summer when the cows were turned out of the sheds and were only brought in again at milking time.

After my arrival on the farm an amazing number of callers from the district came on all sorts of excuses to have a sight of Mr. Kneen's latest acquisition. Being a noted breeder of livestock and an excellent farmer, his neighbours were curious to discover what his new venture – a Land Girl – would turn out to be.

As I became accustomed to the routine of the yard I was left in charge of it when the men were in the fields, or were returning help on 'mill days' when the threshing equipment was in the district.

The first winter was the hardest when I had to suffer the agony of cracked fingers, aching muscles and tired limbs, the results of long hours of labour on the yard, or in the fields in all weathers. Many was the time I landed, face down in a barrow-load of muck, on a wet or frosty morning when I lost my footing on the sharply-rising, slippery midden planks. But at least it was warm!

I'll never forget the first time I was sent to trim mangolds. Being a member of the beet family their roots could not be docked off like a turnip as the flesh could bleed. The soil adhering to the crop had to be carefully trimmed away, and through my lack of experience with a docker my hands seemed to freeze up to the elbows. Never before had I felt so numb with the cold – there had been a heavy ground frost the night before and the moisture on the leaves had frozen solid.

In the midst of my aching misery I looked towards North Barrule glistening in the wintry sunshine and thought, 'Oh well home is not so far away!' After an hour or so I got into the swing of things, and eventually became quite adept at the job.

It was not until late spring of 1942 that we were issued with the official WLA uniform. Until that time I had made do with my father's cut-down bib-and-brace overalls and any other garments that I could utilise. As he was a tall man and I a mere 5ft. 3 ins., I must have presented a comical figure.

Our working clothes were made up of wellies, brown leather boots, khaki bib-and-brace overalls with a belted khaki stock coat, short-sleeved beige shirts and long beige woollen socks.

Our walking-out issue consisted of baggy fawn riding breeches, shirts, a bottle green, long-sleeved, v-necked pullover, green tie, donkey-brown three-quarter length great coat, donkey-brown felt hat with the WLA badge and one pair of brown leather walking shoes. To help out with our clothing problems we were entitled to 10 supplementary coupons per year for heavy industrial work. Otherwise our ration was the same as everyone else's.

In those days, if we got wet out in the fields we worked ourselves dry. If we cut ourselves docking turnips, or doing any other job, there was no question of a tetanus injection. Rather the wound was allowed to bleed taking any germs out, before a rag or a hanky was wound around it. We did a tough job and we had to be tough to cope.

Any girl who 'lived-in' on a farm was paid 18/- (90p) per week. Over and above that she received full board, which was valued at £1.2s. (£1.10). The number of hours to be worked in a fortnight was officially 109, making our rate of pay less than 1/- (5p) per hour. But any country-dweller knows that if there's a job of work on hand which relies on the weather, then all help available works on until that job is finished, with no regard for overtime or recompense for the extra hours put in.

We were luckier than the mobile squads which were formed later, in that we received three solid main meals a day and two 'lunches' (mid-morning and afternoon tea breaks), brought to us wherever we happened to be working. The mobile girls left their billet at Peel or Lezayre Lodge early in the morning to travel to their work, with only a packed lunch of sandwiches for their midday meal.

Some farmers would offer the hospitality of a morning or afternoon break with refreshments, but often the girls were treated shabbily, receiving less consideration than some of the foreign internees who

Laura proudly showing off her new Women's Land Army uniform at home in 1942.

were allowed out of their camps to work on nearby farms. The outdoor work and strenuous effort put into our labour burned off any excess calories, and it was easy to keep slim even with the insatiable appetites we had.

On my weekends off I used to catch the bus outside the farm gate. If the cows had taken longer than usual to milk and I wasn't quite ready, the driver would wait a few moments so that I wouldn't miss my connection in Ramsey. I don't know what the other passengers thought about the hold-up.

I saved hard for about a year and a half, and was able to buy a new bicycle from the Laxey firm of A. & R. Caine for £19, but I have a feeling that my parents chipped in to make it possible. After that I cycled the 19 miles home to Lonan.

Each season on the farm brought its regular type of work. In the winter when all the stock was housed, their food had to be carted and fed to them. Turnips were docked and marrowstem kale was cut by a cleaver, before being loaded onto a stiff cart and being brought into the turnip shed.

If the kale was cut in the rain, the leaves would hold the water and the person feeding it to the cows on the following mornings would be sure to be soaked even though the weather outside was dry by then. I did most of the kale cutting, carting and feeding so I had most of the wettings!

There were two horses on the farm – Barney, a huge Shire with hooves to match, and Kate, little more than a float pony but more willing to work and easier to handle. Backing Barney into the shed with a full load of turnips to kick was hazardous. More often than not he landed his unshod front hoof on my size five – an injury that could not be shrugged aside lightly.

It proved that Louie was a master of his craft when he regularly worked the fields to perfection. His ploughing and ridging, with the ill-assorted pair, was a beauty to behold.

In the autumn after the corn harvest had been carted home and the outside stacks in the haggart had been thatched to 'turn the weather', we turned our energies to the potato harvesting. Although picking after a spinner-digger could be quite a heavy job I didn't mind it as much as some other tasks. If the weather had been dry the Indian summer conditions of the back end made it quite pleasant.

After the potatoes were safely clamped in the open sheds, the muck from the loose boxes and midden was carted out to the stubble fields prior to spreading and ploughing in.

Louie would take the cart from the yard to the field and pull the load off the back with a gripling. Each pile of muck was equidistant from its neighbour, both along and across the field, on a perfect symmetrical pattern. This was achieved by pacing a predetermined number of steps before telling the horse to 'Whoa'. On the word of command 'git up', the load was pulled a few feet further on.

My job was to fill the carts back in the yard. In those days it meant forking out of the midden manually (or woman-ually!). Although there was a Fordson tractor on the farm there were none of the present day labour-saving attachments used, because hydraulics were not part of the standard equipment on those early 'iron horses'.

All the attachments used on the tractor were dragged behind and had been adapted from horse-drawn implements.

The muck was then spread with graips so that the ground had a thick even coating prior to being ploughed in. I much preferred the cart-filling to the muck-spreading.

In the springtime, the ground was prepared for the crops, oats and some barley were sown and the green crop fields were ridged for turnip and kale fodder, and manured ready for the potato setting.

We used 'brats' – sacking aprons tied round the waist with the loose bottom corners held in the left hand, and the sprouted potatoes were buried directly into a bed of manure in the bottom of the ridge and an even pace away from the next tuber. The ridging

139

plough was then used to split the ridge and the potatoes were covered over. The corn crops pushed up shoots into *brooit* or green plants, and looked like a Manx tweed pattern of alternating rows of earth-brown and leaf-green.

When the turnips and kale plants came through they had to be thinned down as precision drills were not then available. The 'thinners' crawled along the ridges with sacks tied round their knees for protection. In the semi-sandy soil it wasn't too punishing on bony knees and a few shillings could be earned at nights by thinning extra ridges. The going rates were 6d per 100 yards for turnips and 7d for kale.

The next punishing task was hay-making. The hay would be cut into swathes by a reaper and would be left to dry and season in the sunshine. When it was crisp on the top side, the swathe was turned by pitchfork so that the green underside was exposed to the drying of sun and wind. A horse-drawn hay tumbler would then row up the swathes. Later the round 'rucks' or mini-stacks would be built through the field with pitchforks. Twine was threaded over the top of the rucks, and they were tied down securely and left to mature further.

Finally a long chain was fitted round the base of the ruck and it was pulled by horse to a stationary baler in the field. The bales produced weighed well over a hundredweight, were tied with wire, and were very compact. Carrying them on your back to the sheds from the Dutch barn where they were stacked was guaranteed to build muscle!

When sheep-shearing time came along the three of us were all involved. The fleeces were neatly shorn off and the ewes became instantly trim and cool. Unfortunately the more sheep that joined the nudist colony, the hotter I became.

The boss did the shearing himself. Louie caught the sheep for him and wrapped the fleeces, and I turned the handle of the machine. As this operation was done on a hot, dry day my job was by way of being an endurance test, and in those days modesty dictated that no female stripped down to her vest. How I envied the shorn flock!

The clipping process was followed later in the summer by dipping. All the flock was passed through the dipper solution and held in it for a minimum of one minute. This was a legal obligation and a government official was liable to turn up and check that the law was being applied. Sheep dogs and handlers all carried with them the strong smell of the perfume of the day.

And then came my favourite time of the year – the corn harvest. The weather wasn't quite so hot then, and the chaff from the oats and barley didn't irritate as much as the hay seeds. I've mentioned that there was a Fordson tractor on the farm and when the 1942 harvest was ready I was ordered onto the old bone shaker with the clear instruction 'drive it!'

The binder had been adapted to follow the tractor and the boss kept an eye on the knotter and sheaves. The standing crop was cut and the sheaves stooked up in 10s along the field. After maturing for a while – in which time we hoped for fine weather so that we needn't re-stook – the harvest rails were put on the stiff-carts and the sheaves were carted home to the barn, the overflow being stacked outside the haggart. These stacks were thatched and tied down to await the threshing mill later in the year and again in the spring.

The instructions for packing a load of sheaves were given by the boss and Louie as they forked up the crop, butts out, onto the cart. A good forker helped the packer by placing the sheaves where they were wanted, always with the order 'put plenty of middle in her'.

Mr. Kneen always moved with the times. About a year after I arrived there he had an Alfa-Laval milking machine installed. This meant that one person could cope, and released two of us from the twice-daily milking. The herd numbers were being increased and by 1945 had reached 23, a sizeable herd for those days, and my wages had gone up to £1.12s.6d.

In the morning Louie and I could feed up, muck out, etc. while the boss did the milking. In the afternoon the chore was passed on to me so that the men could carry on with the field work. At 4.15pm in the winter months I would start fixing-up.

Every beast on the yard would be mucked out, bedded down, fed, watered and made comfortable for the night. When that was finished I would start the oil-driven engine which drove the vacuum pump and do the milking by myself. The cows were given their last feed of the day before I took myself into the house for my evening meal about 6.15pm.

As time passes the memory becomes blurred and only a few nasty experiences stand out sharply – such as the airman who challenged me with a fixed bayonet one Sunday morning at the Killane Bridge barrier, during an RAF exercise. I told him I was looking for some cattle that had strayed, but it was only after warning him that they could wander onto the Jurby airfield that I was permitted through. At 6am it was not amusing.

Or the time my pocket was picked in Ramsey in the blackout, and all my wages for that week were taken as well as my return bus ticket home. An obliging bus conductor lent me the fare until I saw him at the bus station and repaid him the next week.

Or when a young bull, that I had raised from birth turned nasty one day when I had him out for water and exercise. As he was nine or ten times heavier than my one hundredweight, I was thankful that Louie was on hand to get me out of that scrape.

What I will never forget is the kindness and friendliness I met with at Ballaugh. Mrs. Kneen welcomed me as a member of her family and in 1944 nursed me through one of the worst bouts of 'flu I have ever had. People were always willing to give a hand if it was needed.

And I'll always remember Mrs. Kelly and Aggie, her daughter, who kept the little shop at the Cronk. Many was the bar of chocolate slipped to me from under the counter above my normal sweet ration.

I joined the Ballaugh Girls' Friendly Society and took part in their activities. Often the cows heard my lines being rehearsed when a concert or a play was being produced by Freda Burgess and Mrs. Elliot, the rector's wife. We even took our productions on tour in the provinces.... Kirk Michael and Sulby.

When 1944 came, the girls who had served three years in the Land Army received long-service armbands from the Lieutenant Governor at a special ceremony and parade at the Villa Marina. The following year saw us gathering at Patrick on July 4th to be reviewed by King George VI and Queen Elizabeth , who were touring the Island before attending the Tynwald ceremony the next day.

About a fornight later I entered Ramsey Cottage Hospital for an operation. My Land Army days had come to an end.

32
TESTING TIMES

'He's never been more than five yards from a cow's tail', was the jibe often directed at those of us who chose farming for our livelihood. It implied that we knew little of the world and were without ambition to better ourselves. But such people did not realise that we derived a lot of pure contentment from living close to nature and the animals we tended.

There are easier ways of making a living than farming, but few vocations offer such complete job satisfaction – provided you love animals and the land. Admittedly there are heartbreaks when your favourite cow has to move on to the great pasture in the sky, but at least you have the consolation that she does not have to suffer if she is afflicted with an incurable disease, as so many humans do.

And when your animals go for meat you remember that man is highest in the scheme of life on this earth and animals are there for his benefit, including his food. So, as in war, it is your life or theirs and you have to accept that cows, sheep, pigs and poultry die in order that humans may live. I am convinced that animals know nothing of death and have no fear of it. Even before a quick and painless ending at the meat plant, they are not aware of what is happening.

They say that men and women look like the animals they keep, and in any group of farmers you can often recognise the cattle farmers, the shepherds and the pig men. That may explain why some dairy farmers have long faces, a feature of most milking cows, which prompted one lady to exclaim, 'My goodness hasn't that cow got a long face.' A farm lad suggested the reasons but it would not be proper for me to print them here. Ask a farmer friend if you want to know, because it is one of the oldest jokes in farming circles!

The cow has been grossly underestimated in its contribution to the prosperity of the Isle of Man. It provided meat, milk and shoe leather to ensure the survival of the Manx long before we decided that manipulating money to make the Island so prosperous was better than depending on its natural resources.

The cow's latent potential has been developed (I deliberately avoid the word exploited) by the skill of Manx farmers to the extent where the number of milking cows has remained static at around 8,000 for 40 years, yet during that time the output of milk from them has more than trebled.

In the 1930s tuberculosis killed a lot of the Manx cattle population. Some of the infection was spread through bad, overcrowded housing, but even more from bovine tuberculosis present in milk.

Until 1938 I helped deliver milk from our 15 hand-milked cows at Ballabeg Farm to 40 houses in Cronkbourne Village. I pushed a handcart up and down the front and back streets dipping into a keg with a long-handled pint measure. The milk was neither pasteurised nor cooled.

There were few prescribed hygiene regulations although on our own farm standards of cleanliness were fairly high because my aunt, the farmer's wife, held a diploma in dairying.

The latent danger to humans drinking milk from almost every Manx herd was that it carried bovine tuberculosis from cows either clinically affected or acting as carriers, and to this day I look back in horror at the way we unknowingly spread it to our customers. One family of eight crammed into one small house died out almost completely from tuberculosis or related disease. They were among our best customers, buying a quart of milk each day. When I called at breakfast time a huge pot of porridge simmered on the stove just waiting for our milk, warm and frothy straight from the cow.

Innocently we were dealing them a death potion. In retrospect I know that our cows were coughing continually and no matter how much you fed them they lost condition. The farm cats were given milk twice a day to supplement the mice and rats they caught and they too developed hacking coughs before fading away to nothing.

In 1931 the Manx Government took its first steps to tackle the problem of bovine tuberculosis. It decreed that all farmers selling milk should be registered and ordered regular inspections of dairy herds. Farmers had to report any cow showing signs of the disease to the Local Government Board, who sent out an inspector to investigate.

If the case was confirmed, the cow was slaughtered and the farmer paid its market value, but nothing for loss of earnings. The scheme may have reduced the number of infected cows but it did little to eradicate tuberculosis from the countryside.

The inspectors were laymen without any veterinary training and there were endless arguments between them and the farmers, especially as to the compensation offered. In November 1935 the Manx Government appointed its first veterinary officer. He was Douglas Woodford Kerruish who had taken over a private practice based in Douglas and covering the whole Island. In 1945 he visited our new farm at Ballakilmartin, and expressed to me his concern that the present scheme would never eliminate bovine tuberculosis.

I wrote on June 2nd: 'We reported two milking cows, Mary and Molly, to the Local Government Board as suspected tuberculosis cases. Mr. Kerruish confirmed our fears and condemned them to slaughter. Molly he values at £30, but the £5 he puts on Mary makes her almost a complete loss.

'Their value is based on their worth as beef at the slaughter house in Lake Road, Douglas. He says that at the rate of intake of infected cows, tuberculosis will spread even further through the human population unless more radical action is taken.'

In 1948 the Manx Government brought to the Island Professor T. Dalling, chief veterinary officer to the UK Ministry of Agriculture, to advise on an eradication scheme. On Saturday, November 27th, he addressed a packed audience of farmers and politicians in the Villa Marina Royal Hall.

He explained how it was now possible to identify bovine tuberculosis in a cow and to differentiate it from the avian variety it might be carrying from poultry, which posed no threat to human or animal health.

In April 1949 the Board of Agriculture issued its Tuberculosis (Attested Herds) Scheme which undertook to test free of charge all cattle on the Island, pay compensation for those which reacted to the test and were compulsorily slaughtered, and to offer a bonus of fourpence per gallon on all milk from dairy cows and £4 per head annually on all cows or heifers kept for breeding beef animals.

The Isle of Man was split into three areas and on May 11th 1950 the south – including the Calf of Man – became the first eradication zone. Only cattle which had passed the tuberculosis test were allowed to enter it.

I wrote at the time: 'The TT (short for tuberculosis -tested and nothing to do with our motorcycle races) is progressing with speed south of the Douglas to Peel Road, but the government complains that in the north farmers are slow to appreciate the value of attestation.'

By February 1st 1951 the campaign was affecting our own farm, and I noted: 'The Board of Agriculture has just made a second compulsory order defining roughly 80 square miles, over a third of the Island land area, comprising every farm enclosed by a line from Laxey to Douglas, thence to Peel and Michael and back to Laxey. Our farm is included, of course. We have already applied voluntarily for a test.

'The scheme is making rapid progress and its further expansion is only limited by the problem of disposing of cattle which react to the test. Around 20 reactors a week can be handled at the abattoir where the parts of the animal considered fit for human consumption are dressed to help maintain the meat ration.'

In fact beef from the cattle being slaughtered under the scheme proved valuable. The meat ration had plunged to 8d per person per week in the UK, but thanks to this source of beef the Isle of Man's weekly ration climbed to 1/4d worth.

On April 11th we had our first test. I reported three days later, when the result could be read from any lumps cows had developed at the injection point

A recent Freisian Show and Sale at St John's Mart. Pictured left to right are Edna Callow, Judge, John Quayle, Glenlough, Union Mills, Frank Cain, Camlork, Braddan and Richard Quayle, Glenlough with the non-pedigree champions.

made by the vet, that we were well pleased. Sixteen of the older animals, all milking cows, had failed out of our total of 39 but all the young stock, our future herd, had passed.

On the same day as I recorded that momentous day on the farm I found room in my diary for the news that at the dinner of the Isle of Man Agricultural Society, our president Deemster Ramsey Johnson announced that King George VI had graciously bestowed upon the society the title of Royal Manx.

But the press headlines were provided by Charles Kerruish, MHK for Garff, who, in an outspoken speech at the dinner attacked the dictatorship of farmers by a certain element in Government Office. The future President of Tynwald vehemently condemned the agricultural division, and called for the vesting of more control of the farming industry in the Board of Agriculture of which he was a member.

May 16th 1951 was one of the saddest days of my life, and here is how I described it: 'Twelve of our 15 milking cows, every one a friend, are collected for slaughter in another effort to establish a tuberculosis-free herd. Two other cows which reacted to the government test are left with us to supply milk for the house and to feed the calves we are rearing. We still have 24 young stock and one older cow, which passed the test despite being housed alongside those that failed. It is sad to see some of our old faithfuls making their last journey.'

After more testing and thorough disinfection, including much scrubbing of the premises, we were granted the status of a supervised herd. This enabled us to sell some store cattle to other farmers. On May 21st we were given a licence to offer three bullocks at auction in Ramsey Mart. They made a total of £105, equivalent to £5 per hundredweight in a buoyant trade boosted by the scarcity of cattle following so much slaughtering.

The money went towards buying dairy cows to replace those killed after failing the tuberculosis test. In Ramsey Mart we bought a Shorthorn cow, a huge light roan sold by Edward Parsons of Laxey, for £60. There was no question of looking for any other breed. Shorthorns were preferred by most Manx farmers to those 'hat racks of Friesians' which were just beginning to appear.

'We now have eight milking cows, seven purchased on the Island, and Bunty who passed the test and was left with us. They are all of a good type and have been bought without paying ridiculous prices. We hope to purchase 10 more in autumn whenever we come across a cow at a reasonable price. This will even out the milk supply as most cows are offered for sale in calf or newly calved.'

In March 1956 Mr. Kerruish had declared that 1,000 Manx herds were clear of tuberculosis. 'For the first time it is possible to report that cattle herds in the Isle of Man are 100% attested'. He added that in addition to ridding existing herds of the dreaded disease, a number of new herds of top class cattle had been established.

During seven momentous years, from 1949-56, the Isle of Man reached the pinnacle of achievement in animal health. The Island was established ahead of the rest of Europe, including the UK, in the abolition of bovine tuberculosis and enjoyed an enviable trade in livestock to the rest of the world in the ensuing years.

33
BREEDING THE BEST

A bull calf was born on a Manx farm on March 3rd 1943. Nothing startling about that, except that the cow which gave birth to the calf had never seen the bull which sired it – it was the first calf in the Isle of Man to be conceived by artificial insemination.

I went to see this wonder of nature at Lower Sulby Farm, Onchan, now the Abbeylands Equestrian Centre. Robert G. Shimmin and his son Jack were pioneers with a British Friesian cow – unusual, too, because 90% of dairy cows on the Island were Shorthorns. I found the calf strong and healthy; according to those who accused scientists and farmers of interfering with the laws of God and nature it should have been deformed, devoid of the attributes of a newly-born calf, and mad in the head too.

I become incensed when I hear people say that some human beings have the morals of the farmyard. This infers that sex is the main preoccupation of animals, when the truth is that cows, horses and sheep only indulge in it once a year – although our free-range hens and cockerels may be more promiscuous.

Mating is essential for the procreation of any species, and in the livestock world it is an integral part of breeding the best for the benefit of mankind which cannot survive without the food and necessities of life animals provide.

'The bull is half the herd' is one old farming maxim. 'Only a millionaire can afford a bad bull' is another. And it costs just as much to feed a poor cow as a good one. Farmers endeavoured to keep the best bull they could afford, and the Manx Government helped by awarding premiums to bulls reaching a prescribed standard of excellence. It still contributes towards the cost of a good bull.

Manx Government vet Douglas Kerruish introduced AI (artificial insemination) to the Island. The first demonstration of inseminating a cow with semen from a bull was given at Ballafreer, Union Mills, farmed by Jim Looney.

When it was noted that some young ladies were among the people who had turned up, it was suggested that they might like to take 'a stroll in the garden' instead of watching. 'I only wanted to spare their blushes,' Mr. Kerruish told the men. Nowadays men and women work together with cattle whatever the job, and there are probably more women than men involved.

I persuaded my uncle that we should try the new technique on our farm. He was reluctant at first, but when I pointed out that if it was successful we would no longer need to keep a bull of our own he relented – probably because the one we had, an Aberdeen Angus named Magnet of Knockaloe, had twice cornered him and was becoming increasingly dangerous to handle.

On June 20th 1943 I wrote in my journal: 'We have had a cow, Rosebud, inseminated with semen from a Shorthorn bull the Board of Agriculture bought for

300 guineas (£315) at the dispersal sale of the world-famous Wreay herd. Mr. Kerruish, the government vet, performs the insemination in our cowshed. We pay a charge of 15/-.'

But our first attempt at AI produced no calf. At the time, for that fee, we were allowed two free repeats at intervals of three weeks if the cow was still not in calf. Today each insemination costs £15 or more, and there are no free repeats.

The Island has a history of quality Shorthorn breeding and this bull belonging to the Dalgliesh family of Ballawattleworth, Peel dates back to 1912-13.

shorthorn bull bought by Ffinlo Corkhill, Ballagilley, Malew, not far short of the yearly rent for our farm. Neither the milk price, at 3d. per pint retail, or the value of calves, justifies such expenditure on a bull for our herd of 15 milking cows.'

Eventually, in April 1944, we had the first calf at Ballakilmartin born by AI. It was a bull calf – a heifer we could have kept for milking and breeding would have been better - and it

On July 15th we had a second attempt with a cow called Smoke on account of her blue-grey colour, and when she calved in March the following year we expected a roan calf similar to the Shorthorn bull used for the insemination. But instead the calf turned out to be black and without horns, sure proof of a night of stolen passion between Smoke and the irascible Magnet of Knockaloe, who was still with us!

Nevertheless I was still extolling the virtues of AI and we kept on using the service, as I wrote on March 6th 1944: 'Keeping your own bull is expensive and hazardous. A bull eats as much as two cows which kept in his place would produce milk. Few farmers can afford the cost of a top class bull and even those of lesser quality are expensive.

'Top price at the annual spring sale at Knockaloe Experimental Farm in March 1943 was £108 for a dairy

was born to Rosebud, our best milker and the cow we first tried to breed from a year earlier.

It marked another milestone in my farming life, and soon all our calves were bred by AI. Magnet went 'down the road' to be killed for beef when meat was severely rationed.

AI was developed in 1941 in England but the Isle of Man helped to pioneer its usage, to the stage where one bull could father as many as 50,000 calves in his lifetime compared with 50 per year by natural service. The donor bulls for the Island were kept at Ballamona Hospital Farm, until a bull killed a man when he went to feed it and they were moved to more secure pens at Knockaloe Experimental Farm.

In the early years semen had to be collected twice a week from the bulls, because it remained viable for only three days. Now it is stored in liquid nitrogen

147

and keeps for years. Most used in Manx herds today comes from the best bulls in the world and is bought from off-Island breeding establishments. The latest advance is that scientists have cracked the problem of determining the sex of the calf, and farmers can order a bull or a heifer at the time of service.

A dramatic change I have seen in my years in farming is in the colour of dairy cows. For a couple of centuries after British breeds displaced the small, native Manx type – now totally extinct – cows were red, white, light and dark roan, or a colourful mixture of several hues. They were generally of the Shorthorn breed with a few Ayrshires, Jerseys and Guernseys.

But within 20 years, from 1950 on, black and white cows predominated. They were called British Friesian, although the breed originated in Holland. Many Manx farmers made fun of them because although they gave more milk than other breeds it was less rich. 'No need to water the milk if you have Friesians; the cow has already done it!' was an insult hurled at the breed.

British Friesians began to appear in the Island in the 1920s as one or two animals in mainly Shorthorn herds and in greater numbers as imported by the Cunningham family at Ellerslie Farm, Crosby, to supply milk for their booming holiday camp in Douglas, and for their retail rounds with the first milk in bottles in the Isle of Man.

The first complete herd of Friesians was established around 1930 by Tom Kniveton and his sons Clifford and Norman at Bibaloe Beg, Onchan. In 1939 the farm and herd were taken over by Robert Kelly and his sons, who continued to improve the quality of the cattle. When they moved to Ballahowin, St..Mark's, five years later they took the herd with them. This helped to spread the fame of the breed to different parts of the Island.

Soon other farmers were switching to Friesians, among them Tom Quayle, Glenlough, Union Mills, Tom Radcliffe, Ballachrink, St. Mark's, Frank Clarke, Ballanard Farms, Onchan, Jack Shimmin, Lower Sulby Farm, Onchan, John Clelland, Lanjaghan, Onchan and Ernest Griffin, Ballafreer, Union Mills.

Interest in the breed led in 1950 to the formation of the Manx Friesian Breeders' Club, headed by Tom Quayle as president, with Tom Radcliffe as chairman, Frank Clarke as treasurer and David Jones from Union Mills as secretary. The club held the first in a series of annual sales at Ballasalla Mart, then situated behind the Whitestone Inn.

Most Manx farmers lost all or part of their dairy herds in the great clean-up of tuberculosis-infected cows between 1951-1956. When it came to rebuilding, Friesians were the most popular, and demand for them was met by the pioneer breeders on the Island and in the UK.

From the same source in Holland, another similar breed known as the Holstein emerged, mainly in Canada. Some farmers preferred them to the Friesian and in 1973 a group of 17 enthusiasts formed the Isle of Man Holstein Society, the first of its kind for the breed in Britain.

Jay Ussher was elected president at the first meeting, held at her home, Ballavitchel, Crosby. Hubert Casement, Ballakillingan, Lezayre, was chairman, John Faragher, manager at Ballavitchel the vice-chairman, and Voirrey Kelly, Ballahowin, St. Mark's, secretary.

Both Friesian and Holstein clubs were concerned with black and white dairy cattle. They prospered and held different classes at the Manx agricultural shows although only the purists for breed characteristics could detect the difference in the appearance of each. Their rivalry has always been keen, but at the same time friendly. In 1985 the two societies joined together to promote an annual black and white spring show, with separate sections and championships for the two breeds. The Holstein Society's own calf show, founded in 1979, encouraged Friesian entries in a section of their own.

Meanwhile the downturn in the fortunes of

Shorthorns and Ayrshires resulted in the disbandment of both their societies on the Island, although a few farmers still prefer the breeds to the ubiquitous black and whites. With their demise the social scene became the poorer, too, and we no longer enjoyed the memorable dinners and dances promoted by the now-defunct breed societies.

Throughout the past half century dairy herds have increased in size. When I started in farming, 25-cow herds were among the biggest, but now the average is around 100 cows.

Milking 50 years ago was always by hand, and every able-bodied man, woman and even older child was expected at morning milking to help in the rush to get the milk on the road to the customer. A good milker could milk seven or eight cows in an hour. By evening milking, when the pressure was less in time and in the amount of milk in a cow's udder, some of the family would be excused.

Of course the invention of the milking machine enabled farmers to keep more cows. One man could now do the twice daily job on his own, to the extent where in a modern milking parlour a man – or even a woman (sorry, girls!) – can milk some 150 cows in around an hour.

Mechanised milking came in rapidly after World War Two, but it was 1956 before we bought our first machine, a Gascoigne with two units delivering the milk into a bucket. I helped a mechanic from the company install the vacuum line, the machine and electric motor, and in the evening I triumphantly recorded: 'First machine milking of our 15 cows, who make strange of it and frequently kick off the teat cups.'

Just when cows and operators were becoming accustomed to yet another wonder of the times, I wrote on October 8th that 'We had to return to milking by hand three days ago, and have had to do so for five milkings. A fault in the Douglas Corporation electricity supply at Hillberry cuts us off from 4pm on Thursday to 6.30pm on Saturday. The temporary absence of things we take for granted does us no harm sometimes. It makes us realise how much we owe to science and the public services.'

That same milking machine has worked twice a day almost every day since 1956 and still milks three cows daily to obtain milk for our household and to rear calves. None of your throwaway junk in those days, thanks to people like Raymond Riley of J. R. Riley Ltd., who supplied it.

34
MOTH INVASION THWARTED

A tiny moth almost led to the starvation of the entire cattle population of the Isle of Man in 1958. Or, rather, millions of them did. They descended on the turnip fields like a plague of locusts and no one knew how to get rid of them. Fortunately a day of heavy rain provided the miracle farmers were praying for and saved the destruction of the whole crop, although some plants did not fully recover.

In those days Manx farmers depended on 4,500 acres of turnips to feed their cattle, and to a lesser extent, sheep, in winter when the grass stopped growing. But now that winter feed comprises mainly silage and hay, the turnip acreage has diminished to 500. In the 1950s silage was catching on only slowly, and it was after an army of men and women had crawled on their knees in traditional Manx fashion to thin out and weed ridges of turnips on every farm that tragedy struck.

I sounded like a war correspondent writing about the battle to save the crop in my diary of those times, together with appropriate headlines. Thus we had:

CRISIS, July 30th 1958: Until last evening I had never heard of the diamond back moth. True, I had seen large numbers of strange winged insects when thinning turnips this year, but I did not connect them with a pest capable of destroying whole fields of turnips.

Within a few short hours today I see how the caterpillars hatched from the eggs laid by these moths can strip the leaves from the young plants, not only in our field but in every turnip field in the district. An epidemic is spreading throughout the Island.

Control, we learn, is by the use of chemical sprays incorporating DDT, but since the spray must be directed under the leaf application is proving difficult.

No contractor or farmer-owned sprayer appears to achieve this and, besides, all available stocks of the prescribed spray on the Island have been exhausted. I spend the afternoon seeking someone who can help with no success. The situation is desperate if our entire turnip crop and possibly kale, too, are to be saved.

THE INVASION SPREADS, August 2nd: The full significance of the diamond back moth invasion is gradually being realised. Few farms on the Island have escaped the attacks, although early crops, stronger in growth, are suffering the least. In recently thinned crops like ours there are already thousands of casualties, with just the stalk of the plant left uneaten. The epidemic is raging throughout northern England and Scotland, and supplies of DDT are being manufactured to meet demand, but may be too late reaching the Isle of Man.

Meanwhile with a knapsack sprayer carried on the back of our Nuffield tractor we start a counter-attack of our own using as a weapon four tins of garden spray bought from Corlett Sons & Cowley in Douglas.

150

*NATURE FIGHTS BACK –
August 3rd*: Heavy rain is received with mixed feelings. It will cause further deterioration to our hay, already turned four times but it may kill the diamond moth caterpillars or at least wash them off the turnip leaves.

*THE CAVALRY ARRIVES –
August 4th*: Ernest Kelly, my friend and our agricultural contractor turns up with a tractor and sprayer and supply of DDT emulsion to treat all our turnips and kale.

*AWAY FROM IT ALL –
August 7th*: The diamond back moth is the main topic of conversation at the Royal Manx Agricultural Society's centenary show in Ramsey. The news is that the numbers seen have dropped dramatically, most crops are expected to survive, but growth has been halted to the extent where yields next winter are bound to be severely depressed. The show is marred by the sudden death on the field of George Taggart MHK, a member of the Board of Agriculture. I was stewarding with him in the light horse section when he collapsed.

The 1958 outbreak of damage by the moth was the most severe in living memory; 1928 is known to have been an epidemic year, too, but not on the same scale. Since 1967 Manx National Heritage has had reports of 40 individual sightings but the numbers have never been of concern, according to Gordon Craine of Castletown who helps to collect the data.

It is always good to see the younger entrants in ploughing matches and Clarence McKeown of Lower Garth, Marown was the youngest to compete in one of the Mannin matches around 1960. He is seen taking some advice from his father, Cyril.

In glorious weather at the Royal Manx Centenary Show in 1958 crowds watched a dairy shorthorn bull – Matson Duke, exhibited by Percy Cowin, Ballasteen, Andreas – picked as the supreme champion. I described it in my journal as typical of the Island's most widely-distributed breed of cattle, full of character and immaculately turned out.

Reserve champion was Woodside Inheritance, a Hereford bull shown by Michael Macpherson, Knock-e-Loughan, Santon. Both came from traditional English breeds – the foreigners with strange-sounding names were virtually unknown until the first Charolais bull came to the Isle of Man in 1961.

The Young Farmers' Clubs in the early '50s were keen to promote competitions of all kinds. Here Cecil Gorry (second left) and Charlie Magee (second right) display the skills which earned them first and second respectively in the Eastern Young Farmers' Club hedging competition.

Britain was still the stud farm of the world, but breeders of cattle and sheep were resting on their laurels and thought that breed improvement had gone as far as necessary. Meanwhile, European farmers were already producing animals carrying more lean meat in response to popular demand from consumers. Their cattle grew faster, too, and before long took over from the over-fat British types.

In 1951 the Isle of Man had been invited to send a team of three Young Farmers to a prestigious new competition at Scotland's Royal Highland Show, then visiting a new location each year before it settled at Ingleston near Edinburgh. The International Beef Cattle contest was open to national teams from English speaking countries. It involved placing in order of merit classes of the three leading breeds of beef cattle – Aberdeen Angus, Hereford and Beef Shorthorn – and giving spoken reasons for placings to a panel of judges.

The team and reserves were picked at visits to leading herds on the Island, prior to spending more training sessions at pedigree herds in Scotland. Many of today's leading Manx farmers gained valuable experience in cattle breeding through participation alongside Britain's most successful farmers.

The involvement continued for 15 years with the exception of 1952, among the three worst years for foot-and-mouth disease in Britain. The outbreak covered a wider area that in 2001 but fewer animals were slaughtered as herds and flocks were smaller. The YFC international was cancelled because there were no cloven hoofed livestock at the Royal Highland.

Nor were there at the two Manx agricultural shows in 1952, although the shows went ahead with horses, dogs and poultry, as the only livestock allowed. The Young Farmers' Clubs helped both shows provide attractions by organising sheaf pitching, tractor handling and other exciting features at the events held in late July and early August.

Throughout the 1950s there was a vast improvement in cattle health with two notable firsts for the Isle of Man. In 1954 the Manx Government began a scheme whereby all cattle had to be dressed to kill warble fly infestation which caused much 'gadding about' of animals in the fields. Travelling inspectors watched farmers treat all their cattle at monthly intervals between February and May.

Within five years the warble fly, which lays the grub under the skin of a cow, puncturing the hide and reducing its value, was eradicated. Farmers had been promised cattle hides would be worth more if they co-operated but no extra payment was ever made on cattle slaughtered at the Douglas and Ramsey abattoirs. 'Another government promise broken,' retorted farmers.

Alongside the warble campaign was the successful fight against bovine tuberculosis, with victory proclaimed in 1956. Freedom for both cattle complaints continued for 40 years, until some inexplicable appearances of both recently. Farmers who remember the effort and money expended in the 1950s to improve animal health are worried that the Island's high status is now being threatened by a lack of vigilance.

Before the introduction of the Manx Government's Johnson scheme in 1955, which decreed that all fatstock at the meat stage should be sold on a grade and dead-weight basis to the Fatstock Marketing Association or its agent at the Douglas or Ramsey abattoirs, most cattle, sheep or pigs ready for the butcher were sold by auction at Ramsey (on a Monday), Ballasalla (Tuesday) or St. John's (Wednesday) Marts.

We sold at Ramsey where a fat bullock generally made around £50 and store bullocks, animals needing further fattening at £30. Prime lambs sold from £8 to £10 per head.

In 1951 we sold an unbroken five-year-old colt for horse meat at £30. Research that I did more recently on the eating of horses, when all meat was rationed to 8d-worth per person per week, revealed that in 1949 Douglas Town Council debated the use of its abattoir in Lake Road, Douglas, for the slaughter of horses.

They were told that the horses were being killed under Manx Government authorisation, and this must continue. There was no longer use for them on farms with the onward march of mechanisation.

But by 1951 public opinion brought about a change in policy, and horses were shipped alive off the Island for killing in Liverpool. Our colt left the farm in a livestock lorry, and I shut my eyes and mind to its fate. I knew we could not afford to feed it when there was no prospect of it ever having been needed as a working horse and £30 was a lot of money in those days.

Price control introduced in 1939-45 was continued into peacetime. In 1951 the price of oats ex-farm was fixed at 19/6d per hundredweight and of barley at 22/-. Potatoes were controlled at £12 per ton at the farm gate, and milk at from 1/10d to 2/4d per gallon depending on the month of sale.

Eggs sold at 5/- per dozen for Grade 1 and 4/- for Grade 2 at the farmhouse door. Christmas poultry, still a luxury, were to be sold at 3/8d per lb for turkey, 3/- for chickens and 2/6d for geese. A surplus of pork and bacon led to pig meat being de-rationed, but prices slumped on a free market and in 1951 the Isle of Man Pig Producers' Association was formed to protect the interests of pig farmers.

Farmworkers' wages were fixed at £5/19s. for a 44-hour week with £1/15s. deducted if the worker was single and lived in the farmhouse. When they pleaded for another 14/- per week they won their case, but they remained the lowest-paid workers on the Island. Only widespread unemployment kept many of them in agriculture.

Farming was a full-time job, then as always, and we had little time or money for holidays, but an exciting break in our lives came with the TT races held on the Clypse circuit from 1954 onwards, with solos and sidecars flying past our farm down the White Bridge Hill. Now thousands of motorists do the same thing every morning!

35
PLODDING HOMEWARD

The curfew tolls the knell of parting day,
The lowing herd winds slowly o'er the lea,
The plow-man homeward plods his weary way,
And leaves the world to darkness to me

Many times in the solitude of my own farm work have recited aloud one of the few pieces of poetry I remember from my school days – although having been miscast as Malvolio in Twelfth Night, I can still quote chunks of Shakespeare too. But Thomas Gray's 'Elegy Written in a Country Churchyard' embodies so much of the winter scene on a Manx farm many miles away from Stoke Poges in Buckinghamshire, where he wrote it around 1760.

I plodded home wearily with the working horses regularly until the 1950s, when we finally hung up the last set of plough chains in the stable and transferred our faith to that iron horse, the tractor – untiring, but without any of the characteristics each different horse possessed or was, sometimes, deficient in.

My career as a budding badminton star in my teens and 20s came to a halt when I was too tired, after following horses on foot all day, to leap around on the court in the evening. Yet there was deep satisfaction and intense pleasure in ploughing three-quarters of an acre of land each day, returning to the farmyard to feed the horses before I thought of my own tea and going back to the warm stable with its unique smells from hay, straw, oats, turnips, all mingled with the more pungent aroma associated with horses. We would spend half an hour or more grooming our horses with curry comb and dandy brush, offering them a bucket of water before bedding them in a comfortable layer of straw.

By then it would be 7pm or even later. We were expected to stay on the field ploughing until 6pm from February 12th, when it was deemed light enough to work, and getting washed (no bathrooms or showers then) and tidied up to walk or cycle to a badminton match would no longer seem like fun.

Returning to Thomas Gray's 'lowing herd winding slowly o'er the lea', countless generations of cattle could well have included our young stock, turned out around midday – more for exercise than grazing – then making their way home at dusk in winter to the loose boxes where a feed of turnips, rolled oats and hay awaited them in shelter for the night.

The practice on farms of turning out cattle for a couple of hours daily during the winter months has largely died out, now that they live in modern new sheds with access to water and plenty of room for exercise. Often the animals are better off than those who tend them because the relentless demands of cattle kept indoors mean working seven days a week on every farm.

Of course Gray's 'plow-man' has now become a ploughman; only the Americans retain the old Anglo-Saxon spelling of man's primary implement of cultivation.

Today the plough is pulled by a high-powered tractor, the driver rarely leaves his seat, and he comes home more fully acquainted with the affairs of the wide world than his plodding predecessors knew in a lifetime, thanks to the miracle of an in-cab radio.

Although we did not fully realise what momentous times for agriculture we were living in, I was anxious that some relics from the past should be preserved and on October 23rd 1957 I took two old farm implements to the Manx Museum. One was an ancient, single-row seed drill of doubtful vintage, found in a loft. It had one handle missing but was otherwise in working order. 'A similar machine is already on exhibition there, but ours was gladly received,' I recorded on my return. The other legacy from primitive farming was a large flat stone, pierced to allow it to be pulled by a horse as a ridge crusher.

The year 1958 marked radical changes in crop production on our farm. Two implements, the hay rake and the manure distributor, both made by the firm of Bamford, were converted from horse to tractor draught by removing the shafts and replacing them with a hitch by which they could be attached to the drawbar of a tractor.

From Frank Clarke, Ballanard Farms, we borrowed a machine which could be picked up and lowered by the hydraulic arms on the rear of our Nuffield tractor. The discs on the machine cut out the weed in ridges of turnips and kale, and saved a man and a horse walking up each individual ridge. This ingenious invention spanned two ridges and could be operated effortlessly from the convenience of the tractor seat.

My uncle agreed to hire a combine harvester for the 1958 harvest, on the understanding that we would still cut the two fields undersown with grass with the binder. 'I'm not having that monstrosity cutting up the grass and leaving almighty ruts!' he declared.

In the seven-course rotation of crops imposed on tenant farmers under archaic Manx farm leases, the cornfield had to be sown with grass as well as grain in the third of the seven years. The young tender grass

was already established at the time of harvesting the corn and needed disturbing as little as possible.

John Clague of Ballavarran, Lonan, a friend and best man at my wedding in 1951, had acquired a Viking self-propelled combine made in Sweden. With Peter Dale at the helm, the first combine (some people called it a harvester/thresher because it did both operations at the same time) to be seen at Ballakilmartin began work in a field of oats on September 16th 1958.

But in those early days of experimenting with a new technology we had started too soon. The grain refused to leave the straw at the threshing part of combining and the outfit had to pull out of the field. A fortnight later, however, the crop had ripened and the job was completed.

No amount of persuasion could convince my uncle to use the combine harvester on the remaining 15 acres and our harvest, in 1958 and for some years to come, was a mix of the old and the new; neatly-trimmed stubble with rows of straw in some fields, sentinels of stooks of sheaves in the rest. Today the scene would be comical. Then it was quite normal in the countryside, with many farmers suspicious of drastic changes in their methods and loath to adopt them.

We needed a machine to ruffle up the straw as it lay in a swathe after it was disgorged by the combine and row it up again for the pick-up bailer. Until then there had been enough staff around to turn hay in the swathe with a pitchfork apiece. Now the increasing speed of harvest and more land to cover meant hand labour was no longer adequate, and certainly no longer plentiful.

I was sent to buy a new hay-turner, an implement we have never possessed before, and wrote on October 1st 1958: 'When I called at Corlett Sons & Cowley's shop on North Quay, Douglas, to inquire the cost and delivery date of a new hay and straw turner, I was put on the track of a good second-hand Massey Harris Dickie model, which the owner wished to change for one quicker to move from farm to farm in his agricultural contracting business. New this spring, the machine appears in perfect condition when Uncle Jim later goes to Close Clarke, Ballamodha, to inspect it. He bargains with Norman Glassey, the owner, and buys it for £57, a snip when one considers the new price is £73.' The next day I was sent with a tractor and trailer to bring home the latest addition to our slowly-growing number of implements for tractor rather than horse draught.

In addition to the corn we needed to harvest four acres of potatoes, all part of the mixed farming system in which Manx farmers produced something of everything. On December 1st 1958 we still had three acres to take up in the field and store in the buildings for sale throughout the winter. Again, mechanisation was on hand to speed up the operation and make life easier.

On December 4th I recorded: 'The first complete potato harvester to come to the Isle of Man has been taking up our potatoes this week. It is a Whitsed and scoops up a ridge onto a conveyor where a man each side separates the potatoes from the soil and stones, and delivers them to an accompanying trailer pulled by a tractor.

'It is owned by Norman McCubbin of Ballaslig, Braddan, and operated by his two sons, Allen and Lenny. It has been working successfully on contract work. In our soil conditions it makes a good, although slow, job of harvesting the remainder of our crop despite a thick cover of grass and weed in the ridges.

'While it is working here, Manx Press Pictures takes a photograph, and I submit a caption for press publication. The resultant picture and story appears in today's *Isle of Man Examiner*.'

Half a century ago we lived closer to the land, so close indeed that 'clodhopper' was one of the more polite names applied to us. I believe one reason why we drifted away from understanding its every mood was the universal use of the tractor and the machines it spawned.

Lifting potatoes was one example. With a complete harvester, we no longer worked at ground level picking each potato as it was exposed by someone using a fork or by simple diggers towed by horses or tractor.

When we drove horses on foot, we had our feet firmly on the ground. On a tractor seat we were more remote from the soil itself. We missed the smell of a newly-turned furrow and the sweet scent of newly-mown hay. If we did catch a whiff, it was tinged with tractor fuel fumes. We missed the songs of the birds, drowned out by the drone of a powerful engine. Some of the attractions have gone out of farming but some of us still retain our enthusiasm for it, as I must have done when I wrote this in 1958: 'Humanity owes a lot to Jethro Tull, who lived from 1674 to 1741. A Berkshire man, Tull was a man who turned his inventive genius to the making of the very first seed drill.

'He noticed the disadvantages of sowing seed broadcast by hand, stating that "it is very difficult to find a man that sows clover tolerably. They have the habit from which they cannot be driven to throw it with the hands to two large strides and go twice on each cast. Thus with 9 or 10lbs of seed to an acre, two thirds of the ground is unplanted, and the rest is too thick to prosper".'

At that time we still sowed some seed by hand from a *brat* (a sack hung around the neck) or from an apparatus called a fiddle with a bow which drove a scattering device as we walked with it across the seed bed. We could see the sense of Tull's observations almost three centuries earlier.

I continued: 'Tull took parts of an organ, a wheelbarrow and a cider mill, and after much adaptation produced one of the most useful implements of agriculture, telling the world "some waste their whole lives in studying how to arm Death with new engines of horror and inventing an infinite variety of slaughter, but think it beneath men of learning to employ their labours in the invention of new instruments for the increase of bread".'

I added in 1958: 'Have times changed much? Farming is still considered beneath the intelligence of learned man as a vocation.' This still applies today, but before long we may have to pay more attention to the problem in order to feed the world.

(Above) Agricultural contractor
Raymond Roberts and his son John
harvesting maize, one of the
Island's newest crops, at
Ballaherd, Bride.

(Left) Forking hay in the time-honoured way during the 1930s

157

(Above) 1960 Douglas High School Junior Young Farmers' Club following a visit to the Royal Show at Cambridge. Back row: Leslie Killey, Gerry O'Toole, Michael Callin, Colin Clague, Leslie Gerrard, ??? , Alan Quayle, David Kelly. Front row: Valerie Robson (London), Eileen O'Toole, Alex Downie (now Minister for Industry), Robert Kennedy and Frank Cain.

(Right) The author taxi driving in the 1953 Douglas Carnival

Have you seen a better garden gnome? The author taking part in the re-enactment of the Bligh wedding at Hague Farm, Onchan in 1989

Facing page - COUNTRY CHARACTERS - top left: Horse discs are rare! Dave Corkish has restored this set of horse discs to working condition. **Top right:** *Rhodes Tate, a shepherd, lived in what is now known as Kate's Cottage at the corner above the Creg-ny-Baa. The house should have been called Tate's Cottage but for a TT race commentator mishearing the location.* **Bottom left:** *Grandfather Canna, known as 'Tommy the Post', used to travel the North of the Island on his three-wheeler bike delivering the post and reading it to those who could not read themselves.* **Bottom right:** *J. C. Quayle, of Sulby, shepherd and winner of numerous sheep dog trials.*

This page, top left: Sheep shearing with hand cranked machine at Ballawattleworth, Peel in 1912. **Top right:** *Bill Corkish, Southern Vintage Tractor and Engine entrant in the ploughing match at Ballastrang 1995.* **Left:** *An excellent example of an early steam lorry owned by the IOM Highway Board and similar to those used for transportation of heavy material.*

161

Sir Timothy Daunt, Lieutenant Governor, invests the author with his badge of office as Captain of the Parish of Onchan at Government House, 10th March 1997.